CROSSING
THE MIND BARRIER

About the Book:

The matters of mind transcend boundaries. East or west, the problems of human mind are quite similar in nature. Our major struggles are inner struggles and all of us know what it is like to have a mind that feels heavy and stressed. Each day brings new challenges and our daily life is consumed battling inner fears, insecurities, worries, anger and past trauma. Our attachment to digital devices is further exhausting our minds even more.

How do we then stay afloat without breaking? How do we alleviate the stress and unburden our minds? The answer is found in what Carl Gustav Jung said, "Who looks outside dreams, and Who looks inside awakens".

It is only by taking an inward journey and cultivating inner stillness that we will reclaim our freedom from an imprisoned mind. And this is where the 5000-year-old practice of meditation comes to our rescue, becoming a powerful pathway for self-discovery, self-awareness and self-development.

This book is not just a practical guide to meditation but a chronicle of profound metamorphosis that can occur when one delves into the depths of their own consciousness. Author speaks with a passionate and authentic voice and the book is a testament to his personal success story of healing and transformation using the powers of meditation practice.

CROSSING THE MIND BARRIER

LIBERATING SELF FROM AN IMPRISONED MIND

NIKHIL DEV

BlueRoseONE.com
Stories Matter
NewDelhi • London

BLUEROSE PUBLISHERS
India | U.K.

For permissions requests or inquiries regarding this publication, please contact:

BLUEROSE PUBLISHERS
www.BlueRoseONE.com
info@bluerosepublishers.com
+91 8882 898 898
+4407342408967

ISBN: 978-93-7139-616-5

Cover design: Daksh
Typesetting: Tanya Raj Upadhyay

First Edition: August 2025

This book is dedicated

To: **Shri Nana Maharaj Taranekar**, My guru

for his eternal blessings on my family…

To: **Isha and Ria**, My daughters

for whom I breathe…

To: **Mira Mukund Dev**, My mother

who breathes for me…

To: **Ajit Kanitkar**, My father-in-law

for his support and friendship during my worst days...

And Importantly,

To: **Madhura,** My wife of 24 years, a wonder woman

for sticking by my side with a warrior spirit…

CONTENTS

FOREWORD

By Madhura Dev (Author's Wife)

In life stories unravel with the complexity of a novel, taking unexpected turns and revealing the beauty of the human spirit. As I pen down these words to describe the man I have been married to for over two decades, and the one who has authored these pages, I relive the stories we have woven together.

Nikhil, a man of boundless vivacity embraces life with such enthusiasm and energy that it inspires everybody around him. An adventurous soul who lives on the edge, loves travelling the world, has a great sense of humor, and above all isn't afraid to be himself. His friends adore him for being openhearted, spontaneous, and dynamic. As a family man he radiates warmth, is a caring and loving father, and a fantastic life partner.

As I reflect on the journey that brought us to this point, it is impossible not to be captivated by the memories that have defined our life together. Life has a way of presenting us with unexpected challenges, and for my husband it was a journey through the shadows that altered the course of our narrative. Acute stress internalized and accumulated over a long stretch of extremely difficult and unpleasant life situations led him down the path of darkness that ended up with him being locked up behind bars. You will know how and why in the book.

The bizarre events that unfolded took a heavy toll not just on him but on his family too. Our family now awaits his release and redemption as we extend our full support to him during his incarceration. In this time of adversity, he found solace in meditation, a practice that became the compass guiding him through the darkest of times.

This book is a testament to the transformative power of inner reflection, and his spiritual evolution that began in a prison cell. As I write these words my husband stands on the precipice of a fate he did not foresee. Yet, In confinement, he has discovered a reservoir of strength within himself. In the reawakening of his spirit, I have witnessed the emergence of a calmer, wiser, more sorted individual. The meditation he now practices and propagates, was born from his own struggles, and he shares his story of healing and transformation through this book.

Nikhil has written this book with an honest purpose in his heart for those who are knocked down by life's difficult circumstances and suffering from mental tensions, stress, anxiety, and a feeling of hopelessness. With his personal story of healing and transformation using the powers of meditation practice, he delivers a hope-filled message "You can bounce back from any situation" and he simplifies the practice of meditation for beginners and new-seekers.

May you find inspiration and solace within these pages, just as my husband found his own healing and peace on the path of self-discovery.

CHAPTER 1
THE VALUE PROPOSITION

1.1 - Is This Book for You? Meeting Your Expectations

"All of a man's trouble comes from not knowing how to sit alone in a room."

- Blaise Pascal

- People who meditate seem to be happier than those who don't. They seem to be calmer, more aware, less tense, less reactive, and in better control of their emotions. This is a common observation across the East and the West. How could they, one may wonder, be radiating such peace, stability, and positive energy in the midst of so much chaos and anxieties of a busy life? In this book, you will find out how you can join the league of people with lasting happiness, peace and self-control. The experience of these inner powers and freedom are yours to claim.
- Converging upon meditation as the central theme, this book blends a wide spectrum of inspirational stories and texts drawn out of the brilliant works of some great authors from the past and the present, both. These words of wisdom from the fields of psychology, survival, history, science, philosophy, and spirituality render this book a refreshingly unique perspective, not just on meditation, but also on facing life's adversities with courage and hope.
- Downloading meditation apps is not meditation. Sorry to break the bad news for those (and there are many) who believe that having popular meditation apps on your device makes you a practitioner already. It does

not. Also, going to the gym, buying books on meditation, joining soul-cycle classes some evenings, or going on retreats in the Himalayas, in itself, is not meditation. Without daily and disciplined practice, and without a solid motivation and practicality to do so within the bustle of your life, you will only be wasting your time and money. In this book, a new seeker will learn about the most fundamental, most effective, and most economical ways of meditating, one that requires only twelve minutes of daily practice.

- Meditation is not reserved solely for people in the East with an Indian and Chinese DNA, or the monks and sages living in the Himalayas, or some other enlightened beings. Meditation is for all, no matter where you live, who you are, and what you believe. Furthermore, we all share the same enlightened potential, for freedom and power, that we admire in the beings like Buddha, Christ, Krishna, and many other spiritual practitioners. It begins with an inward journey, and this book can inspire you to take your first step in that direction.

- This book is a product of my personal story of tragic suffering and incarceration. Meditation saved my life in an unimaginable way and magically opened up the path for healing and recovery. With my one-hundred percent authentic story, I hope to inspire new seekers in pursuing the path of powerful transformation via meditation- one that trains your mind to develop the inner stillness required to deal with the many problems of day-to-day life. Once clear and calm, you will see creative solutions for your problems and it will open up your life to new possibilities.

- We all know what it is like to have a mind that feels stressed, heavy, anxious, and overwhelmed with the emotions of fear, anger, guilt and resentment which is mostly linked to some bitter past. We fight inner battles and at times lock ourselves up in an inner prison of powerlessness and hopelessness. If you want to discover new ways to unburden this tension on your mind and break free from your inner struggles then this book is for you.
- Meditation today comprises a wide variety of forms, types and practices. This myriad of choices often tends to create confusion for the new seeker in deciding what is right and what is not. It is natural to have doubts, and I address them up front. If you want direct, clear, and no-nonsense answers to your meditation-related queries such as – "Why must one meditate?" "What is meditation?" "Where, when, how long to meditate?" and "How to meditate the right way and the easy way?", then this book is for you.
- Meditation is scientific, and it is a part of the 5,000-year-old yoga-system of philosophy which is completely science based. For thousands of years the yogis have probed the mysteries of the mind and consciousness and discovered the deeper and calmer mental states where the mind chatter ends, and where you experience a deeper peace, joy, wisdom and awareness. In this book you will get a glimpse of this ancient science and philosophy on 'workings-of-the-mind'.

- Everything depends upon the state of your mind: how you feel, the way you perceive things in your life, the way you handle stress and deal with adversity, your attitude, the way you react, your behaviour, your well-being, everything. What impacts you the most is your relationship with your mind. It is the inner health that makes a difference, and this book will provide you with the necessary tools to achieve inner well-being via meditation.

- The way you breathe profoundly affects the quality of your life and inner health. Modern scientists have discovered that most of us are breathing incorrectly, using only a small percent of our lungs and diaphragm capacity, and which is either causing or aggravating a wide range of modern-day chronic diseases and autoimmune conditions.[65] Scientists also discovered that making even a slight adjustment to the way we breathe can potentially reduce or reverse these conditions. With its main focus on "Breath Meditation" this book will guide you in improving the way you breathe.

- Meditation has wide-ranging benefits for mental health, physical health, emotional health and spiritual health. But it is hard to convince a modern skeptic mind about something without scientific evidence, especially something as elusive as meditation. This book brings to light the scientific research studies conducted in the field of meditation and meditation-practice.

- Not hundreds of workouts and thousands of forms and practices- instead, only a handful of the most carefully selected fundamental and simple meditation exercises are included in this book, those which work fabulously well with beginners. The greatest takeaway from this book is the scalable SoZo Meditation, a daily 12-minute meditation technique and program. This program offers a crystal-clear path for new-seekers on: what to do in the first 30 days, then in the next 30, then the next 60, and so on up to 6 months and beyond.

- Meditation is neither a religious activity nor is it a copyright of a particular religion or creed. Although it originated in India, meditation is practiced by hundreds of millions of people around the world in a universal and secular way. In this book you will understand this relationship between meditation and spirituality in a concise manner.

- If you are tired of quitting, tired of not getting the desired results, or unable to continue with meditation beyond a couple of months, then the unique perspective offered in this book will serve as a key differentiator, and show you a way to convert your failures into success. Sometimes all it takes to change your life is to see it from a different perspective. This is the right book at the right time to help you heal and recover your freedom.

- Lastly, this book is NOT about spiritual or religious practices - neither from Buddhism or Hinduism. This book is also NOT about the Buddhist mindfulness practices and forms. This book is about meditation-practice in its most traditional sense, and which includes the core elements of: yogic breathing, mantra yoga, relaxation, repetition and concentration. You will see foundational principles and techniques of meditation practice addressed in this book. This book will guide you on a path of TRUE HEALING where you can reclaim your peace, happiness, and freedom from your imprisoned mind.

About The Cover

On the cover of this book is the image of Buddha, and of a bird flying out of captivity, flying free, and journeying towards home.

The **Buddha face** or the Buddha image is what people commonly associate with Meditation and it carries a certain universal appeal.

The **Bird** represents the Self, the "You", but without "I" (your ego, your identification). It represents the universal spirit within, your true nature, which is longing to be free. And this freedom is the freedom from the pain and suffering that a human soul has to endure in each life. This freedom is the freedom from the chains of the past and the future, by embracing the present, living in the here-now. It is the freedom from the bonds of Karma and the cycle of births and deaths.

The **Bird-cage** represents an imprisoned mind where the Self stays captive behind the walls of past resentments, anger, guilt, shame, the worries about the future, and other negative emotions.

The **journey home** is our freedom, the spiritual growth, towards finding our true nature and experiencing lasting peace, joy, happiness, compassion, wisdom and awareness.

This image is my original design and the best illustration I could think of to capture the true essence and purpose of yoga and meditation. With the help of meditation-practice you can free yourself from your mind's captivity and fly towards your real home of an unburdened mind.

1.2 - A Fresh Perspective on Meditation

"...Two roads diverge into woods, and I took the one less traveled by, And that has made all the difference."

-- Robert Frost (from his poem The Road Not Taken)[58]

In the realm of meditation and meditation-practice, I am NOT a guru, a saint, an expert, or some enlightened spiritual being. I am, I like to believe, a guide or a teacher at best. Or more aptly a middleman, one who has experienced the life transforming benefits of meditation over many years of practice and who wants to pass on his insights to others so that they can benefit too. Borrowing from author David Brooks, I'd say "I am a beggar, trying to show others beggars where I found bread." And I have experienced the truth of what I have written in this book for myself.

The central contention, my intention, is to offer a new way of seeing and experiencing meditation in the twenty-first century. In place of an impoverished, out-of-date perspective I offer a fresh one which comes with simplicity, scalability, practicality, and a real promise. I have approached this work with the same sincerity and conviction as that of a research project - defining a problem, finding information, gathering insights from the works of great authors in the field of meditation, science, mental health, psychology, survival, yoga, philosophy, spirituality, and from the religious scriptures like the Bible, Bhagavad Gita, Upanishads and Buddhist texts.

And I have compiled a unique perspective not just on meditation and meditation-practice, but on cultivating an attitude of treating life's adversities as opportunities for us to grow and mature spiritually. Along with that, I also strive to dispel some of the prejudice and stereotypes attached to the word "meditation" and simplify its meaning.

An opinion like “What? Meditation? Nah, not for me! It is for the monks and saints from the East who sit cross-legged. I am a super-busy working guy in the modern world. I don’t have time for this mindfulness and meditation BS…" - is not uncommon, and unfortunately one that reflects a lack of proper knowledge. Many people treat meditation practice as some weekend activity, going to retreats or yoga centers for the weekend or longer. There is a subtle implication that meditation is some "special" activity to be set apart from our daily life.

Many also consider it to be a quick fix for relaxation, like taking a Paracetamol for instant relief from headache. I hope to change such opinions by giving you something real, something profound. In deepest sense the goal of a human life is to grow spiritually, to grow our consciousness, to discover the greater meaning and purpose in life, and to achieve inner freedom.

I don't just want to tell you what others thought and wrote. I include my personal story and experience with meditation. My personal story is not just about tragic suffering and recovery, but also about finding strength in the storm and facing life’s adversities with hope and courage in your heart. I am living proof: Meditation saved my life and enabled my healing. I add my own flavor and insights to make this book as authentic as I can. As such, history is filled with stories of people whose life was dramatically changed after some tragic event pushed them into a dark alley, where they fatefully discovered a path of inner awakening, something which they wouldn't be able to realize without going through the pain and the suffering. And this path would actually enable them to transform their life in a positive way.

Getting to the bottom of things, challenging the status-quo, simplifying the process, and making something interesting comes naturally to me. It's like Google Maps finding the best and most efficient route to your journey. As part of my professional life, I spent decades planning and managing large-scale software implementation projects for big corporations around the world. I have used my skills in problem solving, analyzing data, computing ideas, and leveraging knowledge to produce this work.

In the ecology of gardening if we want something beautiful to grow and blossom, we must have to create the conditions for growth and simultaneously, pull out the weeds. The same, I believe, is true with the ecology of mind and meditation. In this book, I have attempted to create such conditions, removing all the clutter, the confusion, and the unnecessary information that can be a hindrance to understanding and pursuing meditation.

You will find that many books on the subject of meditation would invariably include discussions on lofty subjects like transcendence, unity, mindfulness, inner realms, spirituality, and so on, all of which may, quite frankly, lead to a massive confusion for the new seeker of meditation. These topics are particularly unassimilable by an average western mind.

I have personally encountered many obstacles in my own meditation journey, such as information overload, multitude of confusing forms and practices, which only makes it harder to decide what is right and what is not. I have purposefully avoided discussion on heavy subjects and provided practical insights in a quick, concise and easy-to-digest format.

It does not have to be hard. Everything else already is, and that is why we meditate in the first place, to make life a little easier, to sit still for a minute, to release all the stress and anxiety on our minds, to just be, to just be present, to do nothing for a minute and enjoy the flow of the things as is. The path and practice of meditation is inherently a spiritual pursuit (not a religious one). This path is the path of cultivating mindfulness and exercising greater control over your mind.

And the most practical way for traveling on this path is to begin with a clear understanding of its foundational principles - Why one must meditate? What is the purpose? What needs to be done? How do I proceed? and so on. And this is exactly what is covered in this book. Taking time to educate ourselves and strengthen our understanding shall pave the way for a lifelong meditation practice.

In producing this work, I have borrowed quite extensively from many authors and their great works of wisdom. It has, in many places, my own interpretation of their work, and in some places, it has their original words to preserve the meaning and the power of those words so that I don't mistakenly dilute the nugget of wisdom with my ordinary interpretation. The great works of these wise beings has inspired and enabled me to compile this book and formulate a unique take on meditation. Any success this book ever finds belongs to these great minds, and any shortcoming belongs to me and only me. I take full responsibility for anything I have misstated or misunderstood.

The focus of this book is on “simplicity”. It is when you learn something that you initially thought was a lot harder and complicated, only to find how simple it is in real life, and that you can apply it immediately to your life in some way. The simplified way of practicing meditation prescribed in this book will make you ready and excited for meditation. What worked decades earlier is not going to work in this day and age of the fast-paced modern life.

All around we see that the old ways of being and doing no longer work. The long hours and complex forms of meditation practices are not going to work in an age when human attention span has shrunk to a mere few seconds, and when life is generally busy. The secret is finding a practice which is simple and one which integrates seamlessly into your daily life.

The unique perspective and the meditation program described in this book is drawn from these multiple sources:

a. My personal experience practicing meditation for years.
b. My formal training in meditation, learning a variety of forms and types of meditation practices.
c. The practical wisdom from the pages of books by great authors.
d. My tragic detour in life via the valley of despair, suffering, and incarceration.

The most important take-away of this book is the innovative "SoZo Meditation", a daily 12-Minute scalable technique and program. This is a game-changer for the new seeker of meditation. This is everything one may need to begin his or her meditation journey. The program details are included in chapter 4 and chapter 7.

Lastly, you certainly must be ready to receive meditation in your life, to come to it at the right time, to free yourself from all the mental melodrama, to enable transformation, and to enable healing. “At this point, you are ready to listen to your own voice, to your own heart, to your own breathing, to just be present with them, without the urge and restlessness of going somewhere else, doing something else, or making anything better than it already is.”[16]

And more often than not the need for a big change in life, the inner calling, the much-needed U-turn in life is realized only after going through some form of suffering or setback. This is exactly what happened to me, where one great personal tragedy pushed me onto the path of meditation, and where I re-discovered its great powers.

1.3 – My Incarceration and Transformation

"It is often said that you must go through the darkest night in order to get to the infinite light"

-- From the book "Untethered Soul" by Michael A. Singer

I am writing this book not from the mountains of Italy, or from a posh villa in the scenic beauty of Tuscany in France, nor from some Himalayan retreat, but from the valley in between the 'Two Mountains' of my life. This metaphorical valley happens to be a literal prison cell in the State Corrections Institute in the State of Pennsylvania, United States of America. Yes, you read that right. I am writing this book sitting behind the claustrophobically confined precincts of barbed wire fences and high walls, and this place has been my residence for the past few years. I shall explain my current life scenario in detail later. But first, more about the metaphor.

The 'Two Mountains' is a phrase coined by David Brooks in his book 'The Second Mountain' where he proposes to view our life symbolically as a two-mountain shape. For the first few decades of your life, you slowly and gradually climb up the first mountain, chasing some normal goals in life, such as get an education, finish school, play sports, build a career, earn money, start a business, be successful, get married, start a family, take vacations, save for retirement, earn respect, be popular, and so on and so forth.

You are chasing your dreams and desires in life. You are running around. You are working hard. Sooner or later in life, you pursue your passions, achieve your dreams, and reach the peak of the first mountain. Then something happens.

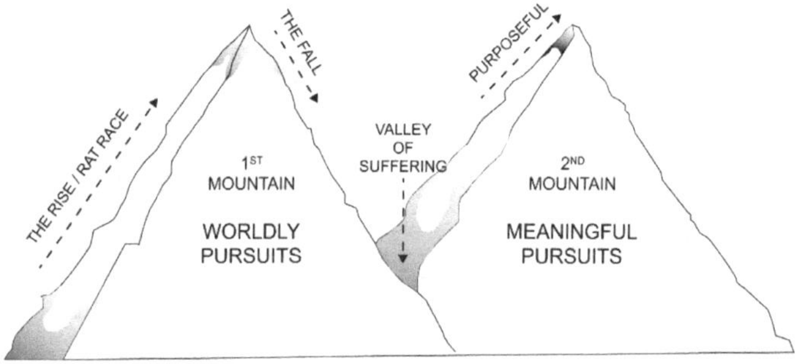

Some people reach the top and don't like the view. They find it unsatisfying, unfulfilling in some way. They wonder if their life and their life's goals have a meaning. Is this my real purpose? Why am I not happy despite being at the top? Why is there a sense of emptiness and discontentment inside me then? For some others, something unexpected occurs.

A major setback knocks them off the top and hurls them into the depths of the valley - a death of a loved one, a life-threatening disease, disability, job loss, struggle with addiction, an accident, a divorce, a life altering tragedy that was essentially not part of the original plan. Something absolutely unimaginable.

One moment you are traveling down the road of life nonchalantly, without a care in the world. It is a smooth ride;

you are cruising beautifully and everything seems to be in control. The air is crisp, the sun is shining bright, life is great, the future looks promising, and there is nothing that can stop you.

Suddenly a collision knocks us off the course. We veer on to a different, unexpected, unknown, and often scary new terrain. Everything changes in a split second. The direction of our life becomes vastly different than what it had been a mere moment before the crash. We simply cannot believe what just happened and why it happened to us. We feel an immediate sense of dread and loss and find ourselves in the grips of pain and suffering.

Setbacks are common in life. Nearly every one of us, no matter who you are, where you live, or what you believe in, at some point in life, will experience an extraordinarily distressing event. It is almost always sudden and unexpected, throwing you off guard, causing intense pain and suffering which can be overwhelming on your mind and body.

In her brilliant book "The Art Of Bouncing Back", author Darlene Santore lists the setbacks that people commonly encounter in their lives, such as losing your job, divorce, diagnosis of a fatal health condition, an accident, trauma from death in the family, financial loss, and so on. She notes that setbacks can feel like tumbling down a staircase with no landing at the bottom.

At the bottom you find yourself in an uncharted territory fraught with fear and uncertainty. Whatever the case, you are no longer at the top, you are down in the valley of bewilderment and suffering. What happens with you now and how you respond depends on your attitude. It depends on how you control the direction of your life from this point. The worst has already happened to you. Now what?

All too often, when confronted with a difficult situation we tend to blame someone or something for our misfortune. Do you quietly accept your fate? Do you blame others for your situation? Do you fight with God? Do you complain, feel guilty, harbour resentments and dive into a depression? Or, do you try a different, more positive approach?

What do you do when life takes an unexpected detour? It is not easy to simply adopt an attitude of acceptance when confronting adversity. You may first go through the phases of denial, anger, meaning seeking, and depression before arriving at acceptance. The negative sentiments like "This is my bad luck… I am cursed… God is punishing me… and so on" flood the mind and it is practically hard to think of adversities as gifts from the divine, meant to teach you important lessons in life for your greater good.

"Some shrivel," says David Brooks, "in the face of this kind of suffering, while some shrink away with fear. But for some, the valley is the making of them. Some turn failures into the very foundation of their development and transformation." You can either waste your time and energy in fighting an impossible battle against what is, or you can fully accept what is, and gather your resources and respond to what is.

Ultimately, whether you end up being a victim or the master of your destiny depends on your attitude.

Hollywood star Dwayne Johnson puts this into perspective when he says "You either play the game or let the game play you." Some are able to radically alter their fate as they look back, introspect, and discover the falseness of the goals they were chasing in life. They give up their anger, bitterness, guilt, shame, resentment, and other negative feelings. They consciously, carefully, and thoughtfully set new goals for their life and start climbing up their second mountain. This is the path of repentance, forgiveness, hope, renewal, and the beginning of a journey towards building a meaningful and purposeful life. This change is synonymous to the Buddhist perspective which says that all of us have the capacity to make use of any circumstance, no matter what, to create value, and which becomes our ability to turn poison into medicine.

"The lion, when stricken to the heart, gives out his loudest roar. The cobra, when smitten on the head, lifts its hood. And so, the majesty of the souls arises, when the man is wounded to his depths." [31]

My Incarceration

As I mentioned earlier, I am writing this book from the depths of the valley of incarceration, serving my long prison sentence at a State Corrections Facility. The unexpected event that resulted in my fall, and I believe my readers must know this, was an incident that involved a fatal car crash in the spring of 2019. It was one moment that forever altered the lives of many people, and one whose painful consequences will weigh heavily on my soul till my last breath.

There are multiple factors that led to and followed that incident - psychological as well as legal - and caused an even bigger collateral damage in the form of a bizarre incident a week later, leading to my incarceration. I won't be able to expand on the aspects related to the actual incident and the case due to the sensitive and legal nature of the incident. Among other reasons, however, the unfortunate event has its origins, in some way, into my undiagnosed mental health condition at the time.

Failing to realize the severity of my mental condition and seeking timely help for those issues eventually led to psychosis. I fought depression and paranoia for months before the car crash incident, and juggled suicidal thoughts post incident. Yep, you read that right. I was pushed on the edge and I was walking a thin line between sanity and insanity.

I will explain and expand a bit upon this psychological aspect in order to give my readers a general background on what was happening in my life then and provide some context on how I came about writing this book. I must share this information because I know you need to trust me if you are going to take the insights I'm offering on meditation seriously and put them into practice. And more importantly, this brief narrative would also establish a reference point for the unique perspective on meditation, one which I present in the succeeding segment.

Another reason for me sharing this part is to highlight the importance of breaking the barriers of taboo and shame associated with the aspect of talking about mental health issues in today's times. People look down upon someone seeking help for mental health issues and often label them as mad, mental, gone case, or insane. They fail to understand that there is a wide spectrum and levels of mental health issues ranging from simple stress and anxiety up to chronic conditions and more serious illnesses like psychosis and insanity.

With a simple Google search, you will find that the statistics about the number of people suffering from stress, anxiety and depression-related conditions on a daily basis in recent times is quite staggering. This includes adults, teens and even adolescents. You will also find an alarming increase in the number of people suffering from more serious mental health conditions like paranoia and psychosis.

I don't know anybody who is not stressed out. In fact, we all know from our experience what it feels like to have a mind that is heavy and tense. We all know that stress is affecting our health and well-being in a negative way. We nevertheless ignore this tension, naively believing it will go away on its own. But it doesn't. And we suffer.

We don't talk about it because there is, despite all the progress we have made in the modern times, a big stigma around talking about mental health issues. People who talk are wrongly labeled as defective or abnormal. In our culture there is apparently no shame in seeking medical help for physical health issues like headaches, or coughs and colds, or kidney problems, stomach aches, skin problems, liver problems, broken bones, and so on.

The same way, I have come to realize, albeit late in life, that there must be no shame in seeking help for mental health issues, which are essentially the brain-health issues linked to the most important organ in our body, the human brain. "The mental-health and addiction issues have plagued the humankind from time immemorial. Today it is estimated that nearly half of the Americans are struggling with a mental-health issue"[67], and these numbers are on the rise all around the planet.

Renowned author Dr. Daniel Amen notes, "Research shows that more than fifty percent of the population will suffer from mental health issues at some point in their lives. So, if you are struggling, welcome to normal. It's a smart person who gets help, not a weak one. Once you realize there are many who struggle with the same problems you do, it will make you feel less ashamed and you will likely open up and seek help."[60] We don't need to hide the difficulties we face in our minds the way our parents used to. In fact, early recognition and early treatment can save lives.

The few months prior to the incident, for me, were filled with extreme stress, extreme fear, and some unpleasant discoveries which caused debilitating mental trauma leading to hallucinations and psychotic behavior. My mental breakdown was gradual, happening slowly over the course of six months of extreme fear and stress. And I had reached a point where I was living in a distorted reality, a world of my own making, filled with government agents who were following me, tracking me, surveilling me.

I failed to recognize that I needed help. Traumatic stress over a prolonged period of time had shattered my sense of security, leaving me helpless and vulnerable in a dangerous world of my own making. I uncover and reflect upon the main reasons as to why this happened, and how I ended locked up behind bars.

Very few psychotic issues have single or simple causes.[60] They often involve a cluster of causes arising out of biological, psychological, social, and spiritual factors. This was true in my case.

One of the biggest stressors was the onset of my younger daughter's mysterious illness where she, then nine years old, suffered sudden paralysis of her lower body below the waist. It started with the symptoms of chronic cough, congestion, and body ache. We thought it might be a seasonal viral infection and took her to an urgent care clinic. She was prescribed cough medication and antibiotics.

After a week of taking these medications, she wasn't feeling any better and was prescribed a new set of cough medication and a stronger antibiotic. That didn't work either and her symptoms of cough had grossly worsened over the week. She was coughing nonstop, all day and all night, and her whole body was aching with intense pain from head to toe. She would cough nonstop, 24x7, and the pain was nonstop, 24x7. The intensity of pain on a scale of 1 to 10 was at 10.

One evening after a couple of weeks on medication, within a matter of hours, she started walking funny and slowly crawling on the floor. We thought she had become extremely weak from coughing, and believed that she would regain her strength once cured. But it wasn't that. It was shockingly, a sudden onset of paralysis. We immediately rushed her to the local hospital, and from that moment onwards started the long fight for her recovery and wellness.

Over a period of just a few hours, she went from walking normally to crawling on the floor and unable to lift herself up. The incessant coughing weakened her physically, and because of the extreme pain she'd make constant moaning sounds while holding her head between her hands and curling up her body. My beautiful angel who was always a smiling and happy child was now in tears and extreme pain, and seeing her that way broke my heart.

Over the period of next few months, my wife and I took her to the best hospitals in the region including Wellspan Health, Hershey's Medical Center, and Children's Hospital of Philadelphia (CHOP). She was seen by some of the top doctors in the state. We did all kinds of tests and scans and treatments and therapy advised by the doctors. She was hooked up to different types of machines monitoring her heartbeat and other vitals. Enduring constant pain, she made it through the hammering MRI scans, the EEG where a small current is passed through your body to test nerve functioning, and many other types of diagnostic testing.

Her condition, however, remained unchanged and undiagnosed. The doctors couldn't find anything wrong physiologically, neurologically, or psychologically. As surprising as it may sound, they threw up their hands in the air, leaving us with a grave uncertainty as to whether or not our daughter would ever recover. We never stopped trying, and continued to take her to other specialists in the region.

We were given a number of probable causes for her condition, however, nobody could pinpoint the root cause with certainty.

Although she needed a wheelchair to get around, we did not get one for our daughter initially because we were worried that the sight of wheelchair may cause her to lose her confidence about being able to walk again, and might induce more trauma in the innocent mind. A nine-year-old was already fighting her own internal war: she had lost her mobility and independence, she had been missing her school and her friends for weeks, and she was enduring immense physical pain.

I would carry her on my shoulders around the house and when we went out to places like restaurants or the library. During that period, I would frequently take her to the Chucky Cheese outlet where she would immerse herself in playing video games and, for a few minutes at least, she would forget about her pain. She would get excited when the machine dispensed a lot of tickets which you could exchange for a free toy or a gift at the counter.

Eventually, however, we got her a wheelchair and surprisingly she was quite happy about it. She found she could move around the house on her own and gained some bit of freedom for herself. She could not go to school as she was wheelchair-bound, and the school had to provide home-schooling assistance.

During this period, my wife and I had to work from home most of the time, with at least one of us required to be at home round-the-clock to take care of our daughter. We had to take her for the physiotherapy and pool therapy sessions thrice a week. Working from home before COVID was not the norm and I had a very hard time getting permission from my not-so-considerate bosses at the office.

It was overall an emotionally and physically exhausting struggle for me and my wife. Nothing worries a parent more than the health and safety of their kids. Seeing my daughter wither away in pain and stuck in a wheelchair crushed my heart. More than anything else the uncertainty about her recovery was quite unnerving, and my wife and I didn't know what more we could do as parents to find a cure for her condition. The ordeal lasted for months and altered the trajectory of our lives in an unimaginable way.

Around the same time period, my professional and personal life was also going through a turmoil. My office environment was quite toxic and I experienced racism firsthand. I faced discrimination on several occasions and a leadership position originally promised to me was given to a junior Caucasian colleague. The office culture was a lot more conservative in comparison to the diverse multinational and multicultural work environment of the Middle-East where I had worked for many years before coming to the US in 2017.

Having migrated from a big-city lifestyle into a small, quiet, village town in semi-rural Pennsylvania, I was having a very hard time adjusting to big changes of the new place – the American way of life, the climate, the work culture, the social culture, everything. Having traveled the world and lived in a foreign land away from India for nearly two decades, I never thought settling down in the US would be so tough. I was already, within a few months of arrival, seriously questioning our decision to migrate here.

I had sacrificed my high-paying leadership career and had settled for a low-profile job in the local area healthcare giant so that I could stay close to my family and settle down in a new place together as a family, and mainly to support my wife in her career-building phase. In fact, it was her multinational company that offered her a management position at US location and she had worked up a transfer deal with her boss. In addition, the prospects of a better family life in the land of opportunity and better education for our kids was also a determining factor in our migration. It turned out to be the best decision from the kid's schooling perspective as the public school district where we moved was one of the best in the region. However, from a settling down and cultural perspective, it was a lot harder than I thought it would be.

Furthermore, being new to the place, we didn't have the much-needed social support-structure of family and friends. We didn't know anybody, hardly anybody looked like us, hardly anybody walked on the streets, and it was a small town with small suburbs with farms and trees and nature. And seven months of harsh cold weather and indoor life was a major change.

Just about everything was in a stark contrast to what you may find in a major cosmopolitan city-culture from where we came from, and what we were used to. As an attempt to make friends and stay connected socially, I joined the Asian Indian association and worked on its committee for organizing community and charity events. I made a few acquaintances-however, the deeper friendships were missing. I started getting lonelier by the day.

The most consequential turning point in my life, however, came a few months before my daughter's illness when I made a shocking discovery which would potentially mark the beginning of my mental health crisis. The stress from my daughter's illness was only the last straw and the heap that broke me was built up long before that. I am unfortunately unable to expand more on the exact nature of the ordeal because I don't want to drift away from the main theme of this book.

I would only say that the demons that had been hiding for years were lurking their ugly heads into my personal life. I discovered that some people close to me had been manipulating me for years and they had repeatedly betrayed my trust. I was treated callously in their pursuit of selfish, immoral, and unpleasant interests. I was quite naïve, in a way, not to see what was happening around me for years, the lies, the manipulation and relationships for benefit. I ignored the signs far too many times and paid the price by letting others hurt me in the way they did. In my already fragile mental health condition, I was single handedly trying to restore the broken pieces and save relationships, but I encountered vengeance and was pushed into a corner. I was literally threatened with legal action and calling the cops. I internalized the trauma and drowned myself into depression.

On top of the ongoing struggle with my daughter's illness this baggage of past trauma and persistent fear was quite devastating. I felt terribly alone, used, and empty. The stress wreaked havoc, not just on my mental well-being but on my physical well-being as well. I began to suffer frequent stomach aches, bleeding, and gastric problems, and had to undergo colonoscopy and endoscopy to rule out serious conditions. Emotional and psychological pain are often expressed with gut distress.[60]

As my emotional life began to come apart, my body began to break down and I lost 40 pounds (19kg) in four months. I lost my appetite, I lost my sleep, I withdrew from socializing, I withdrew from social media, and I was getting lonelier by the day.

As the stress aggravated, the panic attacks and hallucinations gripped my mind. When the panic attack set in, I would struggle to breathe and experienced abnormal contractions in the top region of my head. I felt light-headed and would grab onto a rail or something to keep my balance. These conditions lasted for a couple of minutes before subsiding. The frequency and intensity of panic attacks had increased exponentially during the stress period.

The stress altered my consciousness and the 'agents wearing hats' entered into my world. They were everywhere, 24x7, spying on me, watching me, following me, tracking me, and waiting for me at every turn and corner. This world of agents was an altered state of reality for me and everything about them was real to me, co-occurring and coexisting with our objective world. To me these were real people. I could see them, hear them, and even talked with them on a couple of occasions.

The 'agents' were on my roof, in my backyard, in my basement, watching me with sensors and cameras and military-grade gadgets. The agents were in police cars in uniforms, and they were in other vehicles and on the streets in civilian clothes. The moment I'd step out of the house they would start following me, all wearing hats, standing on the street corners, mowing their lawns, walking their dogs, jogging in my neighbourhood, following me in their cars in a well-planned and coordinated fashion.

Wherever I went, there they were. A whole battalion of agents, employed by someone, for some reason, to track me, and hunt me down. I was under surveillance, and I didn't feel safe even in my own house.

I'd frantically lock the doors and windows and pull the curtains closed. I even did that for weeks and months before the accident. I wasn't sleeping much anyways, and the fear of agents kept me awake all night for days and months. Feeling an acute sense of terror, I'd wake up in the night drenched in sweat and my heart pounding.

I would see them at my office waiting in the office parking lot. My work colleagues were employed by the agency to watch me, is what I then believed. Every meeting I attended, wherever I went, they were there and this made my office life a living hell for me. I would be paranoid all the time and wasn't able to focus on my work. I would sneak out from the back door and drive on the highway just to be alone for a while and find some peace. I was doing that on a daily basis for days before the accident, and my behavior had raised some concerns for my employer.

I would change my driving routes every day. I would take sudden detours and turns to escape the chase, but they would track me down and be right behind me. I even rented a car from a local car rental company once to see if that might make any difference in identifying me, but it didn't work, and they were even more aggressive that day.

On another day I asked my work colleague to lend me her car for an hour and I escaped out in it with the hope that the agents won't recognize me. But they did, and one of the agents warned me that if I do it again then there will be dire consequences.

One evening after coming home from the office I mentioned to my wife, "Have you noticed there are so many police cars on our streets all the time? I think something is seriously wrong." She replied, "I haven't seen even one, what are you talking about?".

Furthermore, just days before the car incident, my wife and I were taking a stroll in our neighborhood when I said to her, "You saw the car that just passed by, it was that agent who has been following me for days...and you see that lady across the street wearing a hat, she is an agent too...and that guy sitting in the porch of that house, he is an agent too...". At that moment my wife was seriously alarmed. She had been noticing my abnormal behavior and my health crisis for months, but she was also mentally preoccupied with our daughter's illness.

She was fighting her own inner battles while handling things at the home front and managing work affairs in the office. Unlike mine, superiors at her office were considerate in allowing her work from home. Nevertheless, when she sensed that my condition was quite serious, she booked me an appointment at the WellSpan Psychiatry clinic. Unfortunately, I couldn't make it because the car crash incident occurred before that and I was incarcerated.

In regards to the car crash incident, in short, on an ill-fated morning in the spring of 2019, while driving on the interstate highway, my decisions in the moment led me into a collision with another vehicle, causing a fatal car crash. With my wife in the passenger seat that day I was on my way to drop her at her office. I had driven on this route a multiple times and it was a familiar and straight road with only one exit to take.

During the twenty minute drive that day, however, I took multiple exits and detours. I kept changing lanes and drove in opposite direction for a while. It was all being done in an attempt to escape the agent vehicles that were wildly following me, as they did every day. My wife had no clue what I was seeing and experiencing, but she was obviously alarmed by my behavior. Anyway, the unfortunate moment arrived shortly after.

The shock and the horror of what had just happened pushed me into a much darker place. When I was at the hospital for an injury check-up after the incident, the state trooper came over and informed us of the fatality that had occurred after the collision with the other car. That was the last blow. My heart sunk and my legs gave up. I was mentally incapable of processing the terrifying news that I just heard. “No way! This cannot be true. What are you saying? It's not possible. There is some mistake.”

I looked at my wife and she pulled me close and hugged me. She was in tears, too. She said "Nikhil, I know this is tragic news but this is not your fault. It was an accident. I am with you and we will get through this...". But I was gone, pushed into a very dark place. Something shifted inside me at that moment

After the car crash incident, I believed that the agents were furious and that they were going to nail me down. They are going to bring helicopters and armed ground units and storm into my home from every direction. I also believed they had turned everybody against me because I was a bad actor who had caused a fatal accident. As insane as all of this may sound to you, this was my mental state and my world at the time.

It was immediately after the incident that my wife called two of my best friends, Amol and Vishal, one living in California and the other in New Jersey, to come and talk to me as I had sunk into depression. I wasn't sleeping, I wasn't eating, and I wasn't speaking. My buddies came, they talked, but I wouldn't trust them as I thought they were working for the agents and that they'd open the doors from the inside to let the cops come in and arrest me. I would not talk to them; I would not go out with them as I insanely believed they would deliver me to the police station.

I was fearful and paranoid all the time and I simply could not trust anybody.

The guilt and the shame flooded through me and crushed my soul. The burden of guilt coupled with a looming possibility of incarceration and other catastrophic consequences aggravated my mental condition causing more damage in the form of another bizarre incident at my home a week later. I was charged that night and incarcerated. Cops were called and I was taken away, handcuffed, shoved into the back of a police car, driven to the central booking facility, booked, and charged. I spent the night, wide awake, on a cold hard steel bench of a holding cell, lost in some bizarre mental state, my mind still trying to process what had happened.

The next morning, I was transported to the county prison, a place where I will spend the next three, and the most horrible years of my life before getting shipped to state prison. My worst fears manifested in reality, just the way I imagined it would in my mind for months and months before it actually happened. Less did I know that the famous law of attraction was at work, and it never fails. I manifested my worst fears.

The horror and the trauma that followed my incarceration and the experience of prison life was even more unnerving. For someone who has never been incarcerated, never been in trouble with the law, and seen prison only in Hollywood movies, the actual experience of being locked up felt like a journey through hell. The shame of being incarcerated, being the black sheep of the family, being the first and the only one in my entire family and friends circle to ever get locked up, was utterly crushing. Whatever little sanity was left inside me was further crushed within the confines of an 8x5 ft cell and the barbed-wire fences.

As unbelievably hallucinatory and insane as it sounds, the world of agents and the terror was REAL for me - as real as this book you are holding in your hands, or the device you are reading it on. The terror loomed large in my life for months prior to the car incident and my daughter's illness and fragmented me internally. I was transported into a different world and I couldn't have possibly known that this world was imaginary, co-occurring with the real world, unless I had talked about it with a mental health professional. And that is all I'd say about my condition at the time.

I mentioned earlier how the fear of being tracked by the agents and the cops caused my mental breakdown, and how I was threatened with police action by someone close to me. In this context I must note that the fear of police is deep rooted into the psyche of most Indians. Growing up in the 80s in India, I witnessed police brutality up close.

The law enforcement agency back then, in most places if not all, was laced with rampant corruption, autocracy, brutal practices, and a total lack of public accountability. If for some reason you end up in police custody or had a chance encounter with a police constable on the streets, then it was almost certain that you would get beat up with bamboo staff (called lathi) and belts and kicks. You would be interrogated with brutal force without any due process, without any regard for the law, and in absence of an attorney.

The only possible way you could escape such treatment is if you were a son of a local politician, or knew somebody higher up, or were a relative of a rich and influential person who could pay bribes to get you out of lockup. I personally witnessed such occurrences when a few of my buddies were locked up during protests against the government's reservation bill. Some came out of lockup with broken bones, bruised up badly, while the kids of influential people were released without any harm.

A lot of Indian Bollywood movies depict this police brutality in graphic detail, which in a way aggravates the fear of cops in an Indian mind. After being held up at central booking custody overnight, I was transported to county prison in handcuffs and shackles the next morning. Upon arrival I was taken to a holding cell and cuffed up to a bench. The special forces officers, known as CERT's, were outside the tank waiting on something.

In my already bad mental state I was sitting there, thinking these guys were going to interrogate me and beat me up. The

American ways of interrogation scenes in Hollywood movies are much more advanced and worse. They might inject my body with some chemicals and make me confess things. My whole body was shaking in my wet jumpsuit. Nothing of that sort happened, thank God.

What happened next was quite unnerving, nevertheless. The four officers grabbed me and escorted me to a prison cell in a segregation block. I was pushed back to the wall and made to strip with four officers behind me. At that moment I was seriously scared of being sexually assaulted. Nothing of that sort happened either, thank God. The cops left me alone in the cell, without any clothes and only one blanket. The cell had a surveillance camera, and I was under suicide protection watch for the next few weeks.

Such was my physical and mental state when I started my prison life. And in order to survive and recover in this alien world I would have to eventually learn important lessons about the written and unwritten rules of prison life, how to survive, what to say and what not, how to conduct yourself, how to protect yourself from the wildly unpredictable and violent behavior around you, how to avoid getting pulled into an undesirable situation, and so on.

This place wasn't a Hollywood movie set and the inmates around me were not actors. This was the real deal. A lot of them are career criminals, psychopaths, drug addicts, and dangerous gang members. The incidents of violent fights, stabbings, rape, and bullying is a common occurrence, and in such environment one's own safety is always a top concern for every inmate. I could write a whole other book about the horrors of prison life.

Was all this, or any of this that happened, avoidable? One may wonder. Did I ever try to get any help from someone or somewhere for my debilitating mental health condition? Why did I not talk with my wife and my family about the fear that I was experiencing? How could an educated and able-minded person like me not realize the abnormality of my condition? Could it have been any different? What if…? The hindsight is always twenty-twenty.

There are signs around us all the time and a lot of time we don't see them, or ignore them. But sometimes we do, and although often late they become the greatest lessons of life. There's perhaps a lot that could've, should've and would've happened. But it didn't. And here I am.

Problems in life come uninvited and nobody is immune to suffering. At the end of the day everyone has to bear his or her individual responsibility for whatever happens in life, without blaming other people or circumstances. That is the kind of truth and eternal wisdom captured in all religious and spiritual traditions for centuries. The path to freedom and peace is rooted in acceptance and doing the right thing.

One has to also recognize that the law of karma is in play. Whatever fruits you reap today, bitter or sweet, pleasant or unpleasant, the seeds were sown by you, and only you, sometime in the past, in this life or the previous. The Supreme God has His way of doing justice, and metaphorically speaking, for me, He determined that it was my time to bear the cross and repent.

With all the above in the background, I am now paying my dues behind the prison walls with a deep sense of remorse in my heart. I have accepted full responsibility for my actions and non-actions, and for the consequences that followed for both the victim and my family.

Whether or not the case goes to trial, whether or not I plead guilty, and whether or not I get convicted, much more important than these questions at the time was the fact that "what" happened, the tragic consequence, the fatality, is more consequential than "why" it happened. And for that alone, I must bear full responsibility and acknowledge the full impact of the event.

I pleaded guilty, and I have done so with utmost sincerity. The lawyers offered me a negotiated choice, a 'plea deal' as it is called in legal terms, and I made an informed decision. My paid lawyers presented a limited choice before me and my family, and advised against taking it to trial. In the courts system here it is quite common for the lawyers, both the DA's office and the defense attorneys, to settle the case with a plea bargain and avoid all the hard work of going to the trial.

In my lawyer's opinion if I lose the trial then the sentencing could arguably be much worse, time in decades. Furthermore, given my ethnicity, skin color, and non-citizen GC status, there were several other factors that could go against me in a jury trial, and where twelve unknown people, with their biases, decide your fate. My lawyers amplified the risks and scared my family with the worst-case scenarios. And although I felt confident about taking the case to trial based on my truth and my own extensive law library research on related cases, my wife won't support my decision. She was worried that I might get a long sentence, and that the trial with its messy nature might unearth some unpleasant aspects of personal life.

Taking into consideration the various risks associated with the trial that were presented to us by my lawyers, including a certain deportation no matter what, my wife and my family wanted me to take the plea deal. We were in a foreign country, with scarce resources, without any support system in place, and it was our first time in life dealing with the law enforcement, courts, and lawyers. We didn't know what to expect and then uncertainty of the whole process was unnerving. The decision wasn't easy. But it was necessary.

At this point, at the time of writing this book and beyond, my intent and my duty is to do my time with dignity, with a deep sense of respect for the justice system of the land, with remorse in my heart, in fear of God, and keeping the hope alive in my heart of reuniting with my family when the time is right.

Months before the incident happened, I thought I was on the top of the world, atop my first mountain, living a successful life as measured by our popular culture – a stable and loving family, wife, kids, friends, money, cars, a nice house, social status, respect, and so on. I was always a very outgoing and social person, and I had a large number of friends and community connections.

While living in the Middle-East for nearly two decades, I was deeply involved in facilitating community support services and organizing cultural events for the Asian Indian population. I worked in close coordination with the Indian Embassy. And as the leader of one such organization, I had the privilege of meeting with the then President of India, Dr. Abdul Kalam, during his visit to the UAE.

I migrated to the US in hope for a better life, to support my wife's career aspirations, and secure better education for our kids. Destiny brought me to the US in 2017 and subsequently to prison in 2019. In one moment, I was dragged down from a state of abundance to a state of nothingness, bringing me to a screeching halt at the gates of hell.

That is, in summary, the story of my incarceration, and I'll stop it at that. God gave me courage to open up this way to my readers, to the world at large, and share my story. I didn't write to gain your sympathy, but I wrote to gain your trust and understanding so that you may find value in my insights presented in the book. It is now time I tell you about my recovery, how I was saved from insanity, and how my mental health rebounded with the power of practicing meditation. It wasn't just an ordinary recovery, but it was a powerful and profound inner transformation.

My Recovery and How Meditation Saved My Life

"Real transformation begins when you embrace your problems as agents for growth."

From the book "Untethered Soul" by Michael A. Singer

The renowned author Viktor Frankl, who survived the German concentration camp, says, "There is nothing in the world that would so effectively help one to survive even in the worst conditions as the knowledge that there is a meaning in one's life." I had none left after my fall. I had lost all the hope and all the meaning in my life. I felt abandoned and lonely.

To survive thereafter I had to "find meaning" for myself. And for being able to find my life's meaning and respond to existential crises, I first and foremost needed to regain control over my mind and my mental health. I needed to connect back to the real world and become able to think clear thoughts.

I was on the verge of actual insanity, and facing the darkest days of my life in prison without any contact with my family and the outside world. This created a deadlock situation, as you can imagine, and only a miracle of some sort could save me from insanity. And a miracle did happen.

It's tough to articulate but I'll keep it succinct. Mainly driven by meditation practice and spiritual guidance, my recovery was also enabled by the aspects of practical wisdom and emotional support from my family. And I ultimately discovered for myself that a prison house can be transformed into a house of healing.

On the religious and spiritual side, the first thing I did was, I started praying. In crisis most of us reach out to the God of our belief and we seek help. We pray and we ask for help. We ask to understand the meaning of our suffering and ask for the courage to get through the tough times. We ask for forgiveness and deliverance from the painful situation.

While dealing with all the grave uncertainties - not knowing what to expect, what's going to happen, the case, the court dates, lawyers, filing motions, separation from loved ones and so on- I surrendered my will to God's will, handed Him all my worries and trusted Him to direct my life. Laying down your arms, your worries, pain, desires, mistakes, and saying you are sorry, surrendering, realizing you've been on the wrong road, (quite literally so for me), and getting ready to start from the place of acceptance and courage, was the kind of calling I was guided towards.

In my prayers and meditation, I was reminded what my Guru always preached:

a. HE gives us courage to face our responsibilities honestly and not run away
b. HE gives us wisdom to understand the situation
c. HE gives us strength to do what we must
d. HE gives us faith to trust him to do the rest

On the spiritual side, I experienced a universal force guiding me, giving me strength, giving me a sense of hope in my hopeless situation, and telling me that this is all temporary and it shall pass. It wasn't anything like a big "aha" moment, an enlightenment with dazzling lights and flying angels, or a heavenly abode kind of a thing. It was gentle. It was like a mother waking up her sleeping child, caressing her hand over the child's head with love and care.

I had a new instinct of God's presence in my life. As it's said when you are in most pain you are closest to God. I heard the voice saying "It's going to be alright. Keep faith. It's not your fault. This punishment is some debt that you owe from another life, and you will be free once it is paid out. This shall pass. This is temporary. Keep faith. Get up and take control of your life. Good days are coming. I am with you, and you must put your trust in me."

I didn't really know what to do with these insights, but it felt like a turning point. My consciousness was slowly shifting. I believe this blessing was not of my making, but born out of the good deeds of my parents who devoted their life in serving less fortunate people and in a lifelong devotion to God and our Guru. I was somehow receiving the benefits of their work in times of great crisis.

After having survived the first couple months of shock and horror of county prison, and after having received divine guidance, I somehow started connecting back with the real world. I was able to establish contact with my family and I began my journey towards recovery. I started meditating in my prison cell. I would meditate for hours every day. I'd do yogic breathing exercises and Mantra yoga.

In prison I didn't have family, friends, responsibilities, duties, chores, a job to go to, the pressures of daily life, nothing. And in that nothingness, I was able to devote myself to my practice 24x7. Who would have imagined that having nothing can turn into a blessing for me in my unique situation. I would literally spend hours meditating and praying. And the more I practiced meditation the more I experienced peace and calm.

My anxiety and stress reduced significantly. My thinking, my perspective, my reactions, and my response started shaping and changing for better. Of course, it didn't happen in minutes or days. The growth and progress were gradual, happening slowly but surely over weeks and months.

I was feeling more at ease and in better control of my emotions. I was feeling energetic, physically and mentally. I was reading more (books), working out more, and making personal progress even amidst the drama and craziness around me in the prison. The stresses of prison life are of a unique kind, not the least of which is living close to the people you might rather not be around. There is a constant threat of violent behavior. The fights and stabbings are a common occurrence, much of which happens without a rhyme or reason, pushing you into a state of hypervigilant alertness.

I practiced different forms and types of meditation, including Pranayama (breathing techniques), Sudarshan kriya, mindfulness meditation, loving kindness, contemplative forms, focused concentration, and Mantra yoga. I read scores of books on yoga and meditation and learnt new techniques.

I was very disciplined in my approach and practice, and would spend hours learning and perfecting new techniques. I greatly struggled, and I won't lie, with the mindfulness and contemplative forms, but was able to derive greatest benefits from practicing breathing meditation and Mantra yoga.

I am often asked, by my fellow inmates, "Did you ever experience visions and enlightenment? Can you float in the air?" I smile and I say "No. I am not there yet. And I don't think I will ever reach such a state. That is not the goal, anyway. Different people experience different things, like altered consciousness, sights, visions, exotic feelings, sense of oneness with the cosmos, and so on. However, that is not the purpose of meditation. You must think of meditation only as a tool to develop your awareness, deepen your consciousness, and deep dive within in order to experience lasting peace, calm, joy and happiness."

I did not discover meditation during my incarceration. In fact, I rediscovered it. I started meditating when I was eight years old. The culture in my home was such that without performing daily meditation, yoga, and spiritual practice I wasn't allowed to eat supper. In the absence of TV and gadgets and phones in those times, there wasn't much else to be grounded for. I was disciplined in meditation by my parents and my Guru.

I regularly practiced meditation until I was eighteen. And then, life happened - adulthood, college, career, marriage, kids, money, and so on. And for the next twenty years, I have been on and off my meditation practice, mostly off. I connected back with meditation in my early 40s, and now more seriously so in prison - in the valley of my own making.

My rigorous meditation practice behind the prison walls greatly transformed the state of my mind and I gradually regained my mental health. I am not claiming, and I won't ever, that meditation is a cure or treatment for serious mental health disorders. It is definitely not. All I am saying is that practicing meditation helped me find some sense of inner peace and quietness of the mind.

Over time, with regular and intense practice, it reduced my stress, depression, and anxiety. It expanded my awareness and increased my capacity to respond to difficult situations, that of incarceration, separation, and uncertainty, with positivity and courage. It enhanced my ability to see into the reality of my life with a sense of acceptance and greater awareness.

I stopped asking “Why me?” and started taking responsibility for my bad karma. My sense of loss, guilt, shame and hopelessness was slowly switching into a state of acceptance, patience and hopefulness. The trauma of past events was still there, but my mind was undergoing healing and revival with the help of meditation-practice.

The fact is that everything depends on the state of your mind- the way you think, the way you act, the way you perceive, the energy you carry, everything. In the improved state of my mind I found energy to begin physical workout. When it comes to physical exercise, your mind has to be ready first before your body for the hard work. I was physically active all my life, played a variety of sports regularly, worked out regularly at the gym for years, and was in decent shape and form, minus the beer belly. The prison's workout scene is expansive, quite the same as shown in the movies, where we got yard with workout machines, a running track, and a fully loaded gym.

There was this Mexican inmate on my block in the county prison, a well-built guy in his thirties, and a professional personal trainer on the outside working with the Planet Fitness franchise. He would see me doing some simple workouts like jumping jacks, cardio, and squats, and invited me over to join his workout group and took me under his wing. I learnt a whole lot of new exercises and workouts, and he trained me well on using the correct form and posture.

What I learnt then has changed the way I workout, changed my physique and essentially, changed my life. In short, I am now as big a proponent of physical exercise as I am of meditation practice. I meditate daily and I workout daily, and I do it without fail, day in and day out, with full discipline, commitment, and passion. The physical exercise greatly contributed toward and expedited my recovery and well-being.

On the practical wisdom side, I started reading self-help books and books on survival, spirituality, philosophy, religion, and science, and that helped me a great deal in my recovery. From my readings I was reminded of what author Bo Lozoff says, "We are all doing time." Some of us are doing time behind the barbed wire fences, while some are doing time outside those fences. Nobody is immune to pain and suffering and all of us are prisoners of our mind (I will elaborate on this aspect in later chapters).

He also adds that, “For a prisoner who gets tired of making excuses and blaming others, incarceration could turn into the spiritual breakthrough of a lifetime." When you can see setbacks within the context of your whole life, far beyond what is happening in the moment, that is when you begin to realize the deeper meaning of your life. The tragic detour can physically guide you on a path of true healing upon which you could otherwise never have set foot.

Reading Buddha's teachings, I discovered that as long as we are alive, we can expect painful experiences, and the quality of our life depends on how we react to such situations. He compares this phenomenon with a metaphor of 'two arrows'. The first arrow we are struck by is the tragic event itself that brings pain and suffering. Our reaction to the first arrow, however, to criticize, condemn, blame, hate, deny or be angry at the first arrow is like being struck by a second arrow that aggravates the pain and suffering.

Many times, the first arrow is out of our control- however, the second arrow of reaction is always within our control.

Daishonin Nichiren, the founder of Nichiren Buddhism, makes a sound suggestion on keeping evenness of mind when he says, "Suffer what there is to suffer, enjoy what there is to enjoy, regard both suffering and joy as facts of life." His message is to keep a balanced perspective in life. Don't get too carried away during the happy times and don't get too disheartened when the suffering strikes. If you are able to treat the first arrow just for what it is, the first arrow, nothing more and nothing less, and avoid analysis, blame game and harsh reactions, then you would have successfully disabled the second arrow from striking you.

In her book The Art of Bouncing Back, author Darlene Santore says, "No matter what's going on in your life right now, no matter who is at fault, who is to blame, you really can bounce back from anything. The setbacks suck, but they can also help you come back stronger than ever and reset your life's path, helping you reconnect to your purposes with a deeper commitment."[50]

"A setback often leads us to a road that is even worse, but leads to an even better destination"
-- Mokokoma Mokhonoana (author of the Confessions of a Misfit).

That was the meditative and practical wisdom side of the miracle.

On the medical side, my psychotic condition was episodic and of a temporary type that usually auto-corrects itself with the waning of stressful situations that cause it in the first place. My fear and visions of agents vanished the moment I was locked up, they got me already, my worst fears came true, so nothing more to be scared of and the schizophrenic conditions ended almost instantly.

I was also interviewed and evaluated by a Harvard graduate forensic Psychiatrist, and his expert report is included in my court files. In his expert opinion a prolonged period of aggravating stress circumstances resulted in my psychotic episode. The diagnosis and outcome were validated by expert psychiatrists at the corrections facility as part of my periodic assessments and intake process. During incarceration I received treatment for my anxiety but I never had to take any antipsychotic medication.

In expert psychiatric opinion, unless I am subject to aggravated stress situations similar to those before my incarceration, a perfect storm- daughters paralysis, personal crisis, betrayal, loneliness, toxic office environment, the stigma and shame talking about mental health problems, and failing to get help on time- the chances of recurrence is almost nil. Those circumstances do not exist in the present, and today I am more aware, more awake, and a wiser individual.

Writing this book is a testament to my mental health recovery and, as surprising as it may sound, I find myself in an even better mental state than before incarceration. In regards to the psychiatry services, you might find it a bit surprising as I tell you that many of the PA County Prisons and the State prisons have excellent in-house psychiatric-care services. They have a well-qualified staff of psychologists, counselors, and psychiatrists.

Over the past decade or so the mental-health factor has gained serious recognition across correctional facilities because of the evidence-based research shedding light on the relationship between crime and mental health. The incarcerated population is offered direct access to these services and the checkups are done on a regular basis.

And it's not just that. Most correctional institutions offer a range of programs and groups related to mental health and recovery, such as, drug and alcohol, grief support, trauma healing, spiritual and religious groups, and so on. I was, in fact, provided a historic opportunity by my institution and the psychology department to start and facilitate the very first meditation and relaxation group for inmates.

Keeping in mind the institution context and inmate population which has never really practiced Eastern meditation forms, I designed a simple program covering the basic breath-meditation exercises and progressive relaxation techniques.

Many fellow inmates have benefited from these guided meditation exercises and it has helped them lower their stress and anxiety.

And finally, on the emotional side, getting in touch with my family months after incarceration, hearing my elder daughter's voice on the phone for the first time in months, ignited hope in my heart. It was a magical moment that pumped new life into me. It gave me hope, and in that moment I realized how profoundly powerful the sense of hopefulness is.

I realized that my family loves me, my family has forgiven me, my family is not ashamed of me, my family knows what happened was because of my mental illness, my family believes in me, and my family is eagerly waiting for me to get home. I have hope. There is a meaning to my life. I wanted to get better for my kids. I wanted to live for them and be there for them.

Back home everybody was trying to recover from the shock of the tragic event as well. They were worried for me, didn't know what was happening with me for days because my wife was unable to contact me after my incarceration. I was prevented by the courts from contacting my wife since she was a co-passenger and a probable victim in the car crash incident.

The emotional pain of this separation was immeasurable as we were plucked out of each other's lives with such harsh abruptness. This part of the punishment felt like a death sentence for me because my wife had been my constant companion for nearly two decades and now I didn't have her with me when I needed her the most. We were able to contact each other only after my sentencing, which was after three long years of waiting.

Nevertheless, my wife stood by my side with the tenacity of a rock and facilitated everything behind the scenes. She was fighting for me on the outside, talking to my lawyers, and she made sure that I had everything I need inside the prison, all kinds of support, and that I was able to communicate with my kids, my family and my friends. And at the same time, she was single-handedly managing everything on the home front, her job, the kids, drop offs and pick-ups, paying all the bills, mortgage payments, taking care of our parents, travels, chores, everything. That is why I call her a wonder woman who can do unthinkable things.

The most incredible and compassionate support, however, came from my father-in-law who stood by my side throughout the process, as a friend, as a father and a guide. He is himself a seasoned meditation practitioner and encouraged me to continue my practice. My kids were very young, my mom and other family was back in India, my friends were in other country, and there was nobody else really to support me locally and talk with me. My wife would drive him to the county prison each week for his hourly visits with me and she would wait out in her car in the parking lot.

During my three brutal years at County prison my father-in-law visited me every week and he talked to me on phone every day. He was my only guide and friend, and I am ever grateful for his love and for treating me like his own son.

In summary, that is the story of my recovery. The recovery was slow initially, but with the power of meditation practice amazing things started happening. Today, at the time of writing this book, after a few years into incarceration already, I find myself to be a different version of myself than what I was before incarceration. I believe I am a lot better mentally, physically, emotionally and spiritually than I was before incarceration.

Meditation practice helped me find inner peace and calmness. My inner journey has given me a perspective in life which I never had before. The way I think about things, the way I see things, the way I react, the way I love and care for the people in my life, my family and friends, and even those around me in prison, everything has changed profoundly.

I know what relationships are important. I know what matters, or what should matter the most. I feel more aware, more awake, and feel a strong intuition and wisdom flowing through me. I feel genuine gratitude for the smallest of the things I have in my life. I really do. I am more tuned to my inner Self which naturally enables me to experience inner strength, courage, wisdom, creativity, compassion and love.

Although I still carry a huge amount of guilt about the tragic consequences of the car crash incident both for the victim and my family, and I live every day with remorse in my heart, I am not bitter about my personal suffering and pain. I was in the beginning, but not anymore. I now sincerely believe that I had a debt to pay for my bad karma and I must do my time with dignity and a sense of accountability. Most high meant to teach me some important lessons in life and thereby help me grow to be a better person.

Renowned author Eknath Easwaran notes, “Tragically, we need a crisis to remind us what really matters, because we are busy keeping up with things that don't." When you ask people what experience made them the person they are, they never say “I was a mean hearted, angry and jealous person until I took a luxury vacation to Thailand.” Nope! People usually talk about the moments of difficulty and struggle.

The real transformation, and the reason the transformation happens in the valley is where the old self has to die, and your heart is broken wide open.

There are plenty of examples of people who have struggled immensely with mental tensions, picked up one introspective method or another, picked up a path of service, or chose a path of devotion, and came out the other end with an undeniable connection to their human nature. Christ says, “Rejoice in your suffering – knowing that suffering produces endurance, and endurance produces character, and character produces hope, and hope does not put us to shame.”

My incarceration, my suffering, my loss, my loneliness, and my recovery has to have some meaning. I believe I have been moved, however forcibly, onto a path of spiritual rebirth and transformation. And although it came to me the hard way, and when most people never quite find the meaning in their lives until their final breath, I believe I am close to finding the meaning in my life. In spite of the emotional hardships of incarceration and the years of uncertainty ahead of me, I feel a sense of confidence about my second mountain.

"God sends us times of forced leisure by allowing sickness, disappointments, and frustrated efforts.

He brings a sudden pause in the choral hymn of our lives, and we lament that our voices are silenced.

...Yet how does a musician read the Rest?

He counts the break with unwavering precision and plays the next note with confidence, as if no pause were ever there."

-- L. B. Cowman[58]

At my home jail there's a big visitation hall where families and friends come in to meet with inmates for in-person visits. That's where I saw my kids and my wife for the first time after three long years of brutal separation. I have no words to describe how it felt to see them in person, to touch them, to hug them, and it was emotionally quite an intense moment for all of us.

The visit lasts for only three hours and when your visitors leave and walk out of the exit door, it is the most heart-wrenching moment for an inmate to experience. It is equally painful for your family to leave you behind. For an inmate, however, such opportunities to meet your friends and family can mean the world. It's the only glimpse you get of the outside world and one that fills up your heart with hope. You know you are neither forgotten nor forsaken; you know you are loved and forgiven. There is someone waiting for you on the outside, and there is a meaning to your life.

In context to visitation, an important point I would want to note for my readers is that on the walls of the visitation hall are displayed two big banners that say – "I am not my last mistake", and "Don't judge me by my sentence and my past." A clear testament that one bad moment, one bad decision, one act should not be a determinant of a person's character, and that it does not define how good or how bad the person is. People change, circumstances change, and transformation happens when an individual experiences healing, realization, acceptance, repentance, awareness and awakening.

Writing this book has given me a sense of purpose I never dreamed I would find. I am sharing my story and my personal experience of mental-health recovery and transformation for those who are suffering, who are sucker-punched by life's challenges, and I want to give them hope that you can bounce back from any situation. If I can do it, you can do it too.

Writing this book, sharing my story, and simplifying meditation for the new seeker is, I believe, my first step at the base of my second mountain. I treat this as my mission, my assignment from the Supreme God. And I undertake this mission with an honest purpose in my heart. I would like my authentic story of healing and transformation to encourage and inspire others in pursuing meditation as a lifelong practice.

You have the power to transform your life in your hands and become the better version of yourself that you have always longed for. You don't have to wait for a calamity to occur in your life, God forbid, to pursue a spiritual path. The healing is available right here, right now with the power of meditation practice.

1.4 - Setting The Premise For Meditation

"Better than one hundred years lived, devoid of insight and unsettled is one day lived with insight and absorbed in meditation."

-- Dhammapada III

There is a range of Eastern and Western meditation practices like Buddhist mindfulness, Indian Vipasana and Transcendental forms, and several hundreds of customized and improvised mixed-bag offerings in the modern times. More often than not, a new-seeker of meditation, a beginner, is not really sure what to look for when getting started with meditation.

The first step most would take nowadays is to search online: "the best way to meditate", or "meditation basics" or "what is meditation?", or "meditation classes", and so on. The search would likely provide you with several million hits, and then you are even more unsure than before as to what to pick from this ocean of choices.

You see a bunch of apps, books, online tutorials, training, local-area gym classes and a bunch of meditation retreat programs, each one offering a wide variety of forms and types of meditation. A common result of this exercise is, and logically enough, that you download a popular app on your device, and/or buy a book, and/or enroll into an online training class, and/or join a local area program on meditation. In essence, an action is taken.

What essentially happens at this point of decision making is that out of a multitude of options and choices that you are presented with from your initial inquiry, you end up picking one or more based upon what seems more appealing and better suited to your personal liking. At this point you are also not really sure whether or not the choice you made and the money you spent, is going to help you achieve your goals. Nevertheless, you have taken your first step towards becoming a meditator, and that is a wonderful thing to do. A journey of a thousand miles begins with a first step. Your decision is commendable. But what happens next, which although predictable, is a bit of a problem.

For most, and I mean the probability of the occurrence is very high, the app you downloaded is used quite a few times in the initial two weeks, and then the usage goes down to once a week, then once a month and then enters the never stage. The app gets moved to the last tab on the last page and sits there like a sunken ship forever. The classes you enrolled into ends, and you quit practicing.

It is the same phenomenon as the new year's resolution. The start is exciting but your interest and enthusiasm fizzles out quickly. Most hit the gym every day in January, then the frequency goes down to thrice a week in February, and then down to once a week by March. And then never, until next year. That's the reality.

And the same is true with weight-loss fad diets which tend to not work for most, and within days of stopping the diet people regain the lost weight, adding a few more pounds on the top. Such practices end up being either too complex, or too impractical, or too long, or too boring and you don't have a compelling reason to continue.

There could be multiple reasons why you are unable to continue, some genuine and some not so much. I elaborate on this aspect in chapter 3. For now, however, let us just say that the main reason a new seeker quits meditation-practice is because "it's hard and needs long hours", and which, by the way, statistically is one of the most commonly cited reasons why people quit meditation. In today's busy lives we do not have an extra thirty minutes for anything else. Any attempts at learning new skills or pursuing new hobbies which end up being too complex and too time-consuming, are bound to fail over time.

Over the years since I started my meditation journey, I have tried different forms and types of meditation, from different traditions, at different times, from different teachers. And I still remember my struggles as a beginner. I could not find success with mindfulness and contemplative forms, and as my life got busy, finding even thirty minutes for practice would seem like an impossible task. Eventually, however, I discovered something on my own, a practice that is both simple and short. And what I discovered is now converted into the "SoZo Meditation" daily 12-minute scalable program. The “SoZo Meditation” technique is the best way to begin your meditation journey. You don't need twenty or thirty or sixty minutes for practice. You need only twelve to begin with. The concept behind innovative "SoZo Meditation" is explained in greater detail further in section 4.3.

In the "SoZo Meditation" program that I have created, the practitioner will follow a simple straightforward routine each day and perform the same set of exercises (with only small variations) each day, for a prolonged period of six months. The meditation is not a multi-variety show. The main purpose of meditation is to slow down a little, to do less, reduce the clutter, reduce the mental activity, and lower the number of thoughts.

By doing less, applying focus and concentration, with repetition and rhythm, and with patience and consistency, the practitioner can achieve the powerful benefits of meditation.

In the forthcoming chapters you will learn the why, what, where, when, and how of the meditation-practice, and all your queries will get answered. This knowledge, coupled with a simple and practical program, will enable you to kickstart your meditation journey in the best possible way.

Before drilling down into the depths of meditation and meditation practice, I want to briefly reflect upon the deeper meaning behind the book's title **"Crossing The Mind Barrier"**. This will set the tone for what's coming in the succeeding segment, set the premise, and open up the conversation in the right context.

It would be desirable to pass through life without problems, to avoid loss, sickness, old age, pain and suffering, but we can't. Each day brings new challenges and our daily life is consumed battling either the anxieties, fears and worries about the future, or the anger, resentment and bitterness about the past. We are either living in the past or the future, rarely in the present, in the here-now. Our mind is roaming either in the past, recreating the past, or in the future, planning, worrying and imagining the worst case scenarios.

Further, the demands of a fast-paced modern life and our attachment to digital devices is exhausting our minds even more. Sooner or later in life we all discover, rather awaken to the fact that we cannot escape suffering, that our life is a series of ups and downs, highs and lows, happiness and suffering, all of varying intensity and duration.

When you are young, you think you are invincible and immune to pain. As you start growing up and getting older, however, life's bitter experiences wash out this delusion fairly quickly and you realize life is not all roses and rainbows as you thought it would be. Every human soul is given a free ride on the emotional rollercoaster of life and no one can escape suffering, no matter what. From a philosophical standpoint, human life is subject to the law of reincarnation. The soul is perfected in every birth, in every cycle, made pure, so that someday, it can be liberated from the cycle of birth and death, and the suffering.

Have you ever noticed that we don't have one day that is free from worries and anxiety of some sort? There is always something or someone, without fail, every single day, that stresses us out. There is always someone or something that pisses us off, spoils our mood, gets on our nerves, makes us angry, treats us badly, gossips about us, and so on. One thing leads to another, and we are on the bandwagon of anxiety, fear, anger, depression, guilt, shame, resentment, and loads of other negative emotions. In short, we suffer. In our minds. And this is the same suffering that Buddha talked about.

Furthermore, the problems in life show up when you least expect it to and most often without an advance warning. The problems surface in many shapes and forms - you fail an important exam, suffer a major financial loss, get shamed on social media by some lunatic, face the sudden death of a loved one, get betrayed by a friend, be diagnosed with an incurable life threatening disease, be wrongly convicted of a crime you didn't commit, discover the unfaithfulness of your spouse, get fired from a secure job, suffer with addiction and homelessness, and so on.

Amidst the many uncertainties of daily life where problems show up uninvited, having an attitude like "Oh, I'll deal with it when it occurs", or "Oh, that won't happen to me", - is a wishful thinking and a bad attitude to live your lives with. It is not that you should expect bad problems all the time and be paranoid thinking about the worst that could happen to you. That is not my point.

The point is, that the problems come uninvited, and you should be "mentally strong and ready" to receive them in your life. The point is about recognizing with full awareness that along with some good sunny days, life is going to throw in some unpleasant dark rainy days as well. The point is about readiness so that you don't break in the face of a calamity. If you are strong you will sustain, otherwise you will perish. This is the law of nature and the law of survival.

You cannot google "How to swim?" while you are drowning. Get it? And that's my point. Googling beforehand instead, as early as possible in life, "How to develop mental strength?" "How to face life's storms with calm and composure?" "How to prepare for life's challenges?" perhaps makes more sense. Does it not?

The way things are going on in the world today and the way most of us live our lives under daily uncertainties and tensions, there comes a time in life when we get fed up with all the drama in life. We get fed up with the same routine and being stuck in the same jobs that we hate to our core. Life feels like Groundhog Day (the movie), reliving the same day over and over again, and there seems to be no escape from the situation.

Every single day there are bills to be paid, careers to be built, a family to be fed and dreams to be achieved. Desires and attachments run our life. Life becomes an endless pursuit of desires. One desire gets fulfilled only to be replaced by another. We want more and more, bigger, better, larger, bigger houses, better cars, more money, latest iPhone, newest gadgets, more sneakers, more clothes, better partners, better jobs, more likes on social media, and so on.

These cravings of various kinds bring stress and tension into your life as you are working even harder to achieve them. In spite of having everything and more, the sense of contentment is missing. It is never enough. And then, another problem is that you get attached to the things that you possess. You don't want to lose your possessions, be it money, relationships, your car, phone, house, things, status, and so on.

Your attachments become your identity. You worked hard to possess things in your life and now you are working hard to not lose them from your life. You sacrifice your health and well-being chasing desires and increasing your attachments, and you wanting to preserve them for as long as you can invites, unconsciously, more stress into your life. Over time, this creates more tension in your mind.

> *"You may not have been sentenced to prison, but you have imprisoned yourself behind the walls of a conditioned mind."*

At times it feels like we are living in a pressure cooker. There is this underlying feeling of wanting to run away from all of that, breaking the proverbial chains and going someplace where there is peace and quiet, somewhere deep into the woods.... on the mountain, in the forest, deep into the ocean, in some secluded place, to be away from the problems of the world, away from traffic, away from chaos and breathe a breath of fresh air.

For a few hours at least, forget about the daily pressures and recurring problems, and just unwind, relax, stop thinking, chill out, be yourself, enjoy the silence, enjoy nature, and let no one bother you. It’s like - just leave me alone for a bit.

Finding a quiet and green space in city areas, however, could be a bit of a challenge in itself. With the way our cities have expanded into these concrete jungles, the forests and hills and trees have disappeared rapidly. This is especially true across many countries in the Indian subcontinent.

There is a certain aspect of being in nature that provides a sense of calmness and the experience is often amazingly fulfilling. So you escape into nature, say. You are fine for a bit. You experience the peace and quiet that you have been longing for. But you can't be in a forest forever, can you?

You got to get back to your job and the family and the world you left behind. If not today, surely tomorrow. That's the sad reality of our life on earth, unless of course you are on the path of renunciation. And even if you do not return home, the worries and the problems will find you shortly. You won't be able to escape from them for long. Do you know why so?

The reason is, wherever you go there it is. Your mind.

The restless mind is the source of all your anxieties and mental tensions. The burdened mind travels with you wherever you go and it is the home of past traumas and worries about the future. It does not matter if you take an expensive vacation to Hawaii or sail to Bahamas or climb the Himalayas if you are going to think the same thoughts, have the same emotional reaction, and feel the same kind of tension in your mind which you were essentially trying to escape.

When your mind is burdened it will be hard to find peace and joy in any corner of the world. When your mind is filled with resentments about the past, with anger, guilt, shame, and other negative emotions, you won't be able to experience restfulness for long. When you are hostage to mind conditioning, the habits and patterns of thinking that are deeply ingrained into your psyche, you tend to recreate the trauma of some unpleasant event in your life that you are unable to let go of.

And when your mind is not at ease, your physical health is adversely affected, too. Only when the incessant thinking stops and when you are able to sit quietly in one place, with yourself, turning inwards, reaching a deep state consciousness, can you experience the peace and the calm that you are searching for.

Over the Eons of its evolutionary period your mind has been conditioned in a certain way. And more and more layers of conditioning get added each moment from your present-day environment, culture, society, beliefs, values, education, and so on. The way we think, reason, act, perceive, react, form opinions, understand, every other behavioral aspect is an effect of our conditioning (called "Samskaras", a Sanskrit term in Indian philosophy). Your Samskaras become your identity, the "I" of your personality.

This conditioning is the filter through which we perceive our world and which blocks the consciousness from flowing freely. You start believing that you are your body, you are your thoughts, you are your emotions, you are your personality, you are your fame, you are your status, you are your job title, you are your car, you are your house, you are your social media profile, and so on. The real you, the Self, your true nature, remains hidden underneath these layers. And as long as your consciousness is attached to your identity, the Ego, you won't be able to truly unburden your mind your whole life and connect with your true nature.

This is not a philosophy but a fact of human life. And according to Buddhist teachings, this mind conditioning and our attachment to other people and things in life, is the main cause of human suffering. Whatever we are attached to can bring immense joy and the same thing can bring immense pain.

You buy a car, you get attached, you are happy. The car is stolen or damaged in an accident, you are sad. You love your wife, you are attached, she makes you happy. You find out she is cheating on you, your world collapses. You are famous on social media, an influencer, you are attached to your fame. Someone posts nasty comments and photos exposing your affair, suddenly you lose your fame and respect.

But there is a way out in order to lessen the tension on our minds and lessen our suffering. There is a way and a place where you will find lasting peace, lasting joy, extraordinary wisdom, and lasting happiness. In this particular place all your problems will dissolve and all your mental conflicts will come to an end. In this place the desires and attachments lose their hold on you. This place is within you. This place is inside your mind.

Just as the problem resides in your mind, so does the solution. The only difference is that the solution resides at a much deeper level in the mind than the problem does. In order to reach there, however, you must draw your consciousness deeper, layer-by-layer, like peeling an onion and reaching the innermost core. I elaborate upon this aspect in the section 'Workings of the Mind' in chapter 3.

The vehicle, the method, the process to reach this inner and deeper place in mind is known as "Meditation"; and meditation-practice becomes the "Doorway" to the inner realm of an unburdened mind. And the state you achieve is often termed as an enlightened mind, aka the Krishna consciousness or Christ consciousness. This is our real home. Human mind is the barrier to our freedom from the grips of past and future thinking, from our suffering, and from our bondage. Buddha says, "In order to cross the mind barrier you must drop all the weight you have gathered." Drop your thoughts, your emotional baggage of prejudices, guilt, and anger, drop your likes and dislikes, your problems, your attachments, and your desires. This is not to be mistaken for renunciation. You continue to be a part of the world, fulfilling your responsibilities, but you are doing so in a state of awareness.

Once you cross over you are able to stay calm, collected, and centered even in the middle of crisis. That's the meditative mind, an unburdened mind. From both a psychological and practical perspective, **Crossing The Mind Barrier** to unite with your true nature can bring an end to all the drama, cravings, desires, and mental tensions, and you experience the real joy, peace, love, happiness, and wisdom

Crossing the mind barrier is nothing but the liberation from an imprisoned mind. It is about experiencing:

- A world of true healing.
- A meditative mind that is steady, calm, strong, and clear.
- Absence of fear and worries. Less stress and anxieties; great self-control; greater wisdom.
- Ability to face life's challenges, small or big, with greater control and mindfulness.

- Ability to overcome temptations and cravings.
- Ability to control emotions.
- Ability to let go, to accept, to forgive and release past bitterness.
- Interconnectedness with the world around you.
- Infinite power, energy, peace, and happiness.

In absence of these qualities, you will only be existing rather than living a vibrant and colourful life. In order to thrive in your life and to establish a sense of flow and peace in everything you do, every single day, you must cultivate greater control over your mind using the powers of meditation practice. And do it with a sense of urgency as highlighted in the next section.

1. 5 - Urgency for Meditation and The Two Worlds

"Once the cause of suffering is seen, Healing is possible."

-- Buddha

The 19th century philosopher Friedrich Nietzsche said, "He who has a Why to live for can bear with almost any How." The same adage is proclaimed by Viktor Frankl in his famous book "Man's Search for Meaning", where he poignantly describes the fears and hopes of a life at a German concentration camp. He articulates his central point about survival as: finding a meaning in your suffering, of finding a purpose in your life, in caring deeply about something to live for, and forging an attitude of never giving up. Having the knowledge and awareness of the "why" you are doing what you are doing or "why" you are suffering, having that clarity, having that acceptance, shall render meaning to your actions.

Knowing the "why" energizes you to endure the difficult times with courage and hope. It builds resilience and character. He adds, "Suffering upsets the normal patterns of life and reminds us that you are not what you thought you were; suffering teaches us gratitude, and suffering also calls for a response." When one discovers that there is a meaning to their suffering, their whole attitude towards life undergoes a positive transformation from feeling like a victim and martyr to feeling gratitude. Their perspective changes from a place of anger, bitterness and resentment to a place of awareness, acceptance and hope.

So, before we begin to dig any deeper into the 'how' and 'what' about meditation, I want to first establish the 'why to meditate?'- a solid purpose, a pressing reason, for practicing meditation. The answer to this question is not the conventional one, like: meditation is good for you, it has many benefits, it helps calm your mind, it is the latest trend, celebrities are doing it, you look so cool doing meditation and your social media posts will get millions of likes and fan following, and so on.

No, that is not the kind of WHY I am interested in. While all these could be valid reasons, they are not enough to establish a heightened sense of urgency and reflect a dire need to begin meditating. They do not establish a level of urgency and motivation to get you out of your chair and become a mediator.

In establishing the "Why" for meditation I am reminded of a wonderfully motivating scene from a famous movie named "Forrest Gump" starring Tom Hanks. The young Forrest is walking back home with his girlfriend, and he wears this metallic leg-brace to support his handicapped legs. In this scene, he is being chased by a few bullies riding on their bicycles and are about to hit him.

Sensing the urgency of the situation and caring deeply for Forrest, his friend Jenny shouts out repeatedly, "Run Forrest run... run Forrest run." Alarmed, Forrest starts running. It is quite difficult for him to run with braces on, but he gathers all the energy and keeps running. The bearing and parts of the metal brace start to snap off and fly out in slow motion, and oh boy, he runs fast at a lightning speed and never stops running.

In the end, an urgency born out of a challenging detour in life turns out to be a profoundly motivating and liberating experience for Forrest Gump.

In this book I offer a fresh perspective, one which reflects the "Run Forrest Run” level of urgency and motivation in pursuing meditation. What's more, in today’s skeptical times, it is hard to convince an urban mind on the wide-ranging benefits of meditation without providing scientific evidence and statistical proof of some sort. I therefore include, in a separate section, a brief reference to some of the scientific research studies conducted on the subject of meditation. My unique and wholesome perspective, I promise, will be a key differentiator between you pursuing meditation for life versus you quitting or not starting at all.

The yoga master B.K.S. Iyengar says, "The army general surveys the terrain, the enemy location, and the enemy capability, in order to plan and strategize his line of attack and win the war." The same way, I propose we survey the meditation landscape starting at thirty thousand feet, a bird's eye view, and then dive to the ground level to take a closer and deeper look at the various aspects of meditation.

The Two Worlds

My case on meditation, the big WHY, is based on understanding the state of the two worlds we live in: the outer world and the inner world. The outer world is our objective world, real for us, containing people, things, trees, roads, mountains, cities, cars, buildings, the sky, stars, galaxies, the universe, and so on, all that resides outside of the human body. And the inner world is the one contained inside the human mind and made up of sense perceptions, thoughts, memory, emotions, feelings, intellect, intuition, ego, and consciousness. It is through this inner world that we perceive the outer world.

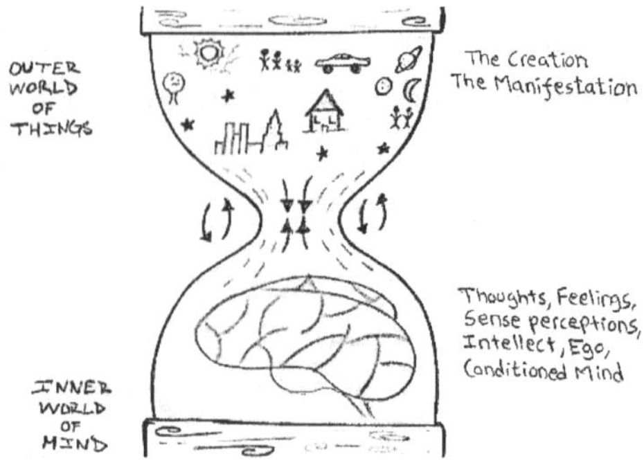

Timothy Ferris, in his book 'The Mind's Sky', invites us to envision our relationship with the universe as a symmetrical hourglass, where on one side is the outer realm inhabited by galaxies, stars, our planet, plants, animals, fellow humans, things, everything that we see in our world. And on the other side is the inner realm of mind where we try to make sense of the outer world through our senses, perceptions and memory- and, in the process, build our self -identity, ego, personality etc. And through the neck of the hourglass flows the sense data where the world ‘out there’ flows and merges with the world ‘in here’.

The world we live in is a projection of our mind. We perceive the world with limited sense perceptions that have limited range and capability. What we can see, what we can hear, what we can taste, what we can smell and what we can feel, has limitations, and is within a finite spectrum. We all know dogs have an advanced sense of smell than humans. Some birds have much more advanced vision than humans.

At every moment we receive multiple sensory stimuli about the reality out there through our senses. This external stimuli, billions and billions of bytes of data, is mixed with your thoughts, memories, perceptions, intellect and Ego. We further try to make sense of the perceived data using our memory, intellect, reasoning, intelligence and applying our mental conditioning.

The conditioning is nothing but our environment which is constantly changing, what our parents taught us, our beliefs, culture, traditions, values, the facts we are fed in school, and so on. Although we all receive the same data from the universe, the way each individual would process this data is very different and is based upon his or her mind conditioning. And that is why my world created by my mind would greatly be different from your world created by your mind.

The mind filters in only a tiny subset from this entire reality. This tiny subset is the things that matter to us and become our individual and personal experience, thus creating "the reality in here". Basically we recreate the outside world inside ourselves, a personal model, and we live in our mind.

"We see the world not as it is But as we are."

- Stephen Covey

In his book 'The Power of Your Subconscious Mind', author Joseph Murphy notes (something that's also mentioned in Eastern scriptures), that those who are enlightened realize that the world within creates the world without. Your thoughts, feelings, and visualized imagery are the organizing principles of your experiences.

The ancient wisdom 'as you sow, so shall you reap', is another way of saying 'as you think (inner world) so shall you become (outer world)'. If there is joy and peace inside, there will be joy and peace outside. If there is joy and peace outside, there will be joy and peace inside. This is how everything is connected and how the two worlds reflect each other.

The important thing to consider in this context is that these two worlds often end in conflict, giving rise to pain and suffering. The conflict shows up in the form of discontentment with what-is, our status quo. Neither are we happy and satisfied in the outer world, nor are we at peace in the inner world. What begins in our minds as imaginary takes real shape in the world through our actions.

The inner world, riddled with tension, imposes similar types of tension on our external world. Some forms of disturbance in the outer world have caused a turmoil in your inner world, and the disturbances of the inner world manifest themselves as problems of the outer world: the hourglass seems to be flipping around into a perpetual motion. So, the question arises: How do we lessen the conflict and establish balance? How do we ensure peace, progress, and prosperity?

The answer to these questions is surprisingly straightforward. By changing our inner world, an action which is totally within our individual circle of influence and control, we can change our outer world. And one of the methods we can use in this process is that of meditation-practice. I elaborate upon this aspect in detail in chapter 3. The solution to your problems cannot be found in the outer world. Any fix on the outside will always be temporary.

The permanent solution to your problems is to fix the part that seems to have so many problems on daily basis, and which is "you", your mind, your inner world. If you want to be truly free then you must commit yourself to fix the inner world.

So friends, I present my case for meditation by arguing the current state of affairs of both the worlds we live in, and how these worlds influence each other, creating the reality we experience as life, as our everyday existence. This understanding shall pave the way and act as a well-guarded foundation upon which you can build your meditation practice, and reclaim control over your inner world with the same level of urgency as "Run Forrest Run".

In order to establish a solid WHY for meditation practice, let us take a closer look at the current state of affairs of the world we live in - both the outer and the inner. I suggest you buckle up. I don't think I am going to propose anything new, or something that you don't already know. All I am trying is to bring some of the pressing issues of today's times into the foreground, into your awareness, so that you can see how your life and the state of your mind is affected by it. And which will further help you realize the need for having a transformative tool like meditation practice in your life.

All it takes to shift onto a path of self-development and spiritual evolution is an awakening, a realization, that something needs to change. The status quo ain't working. And let us see why in the next chapter.

CHAPTER 2
A SOLID REASON TO MEDITATE. THE WHY?

2.1 - Outer World: The Current State of Affairs

We are quite undoubtedly living in an era of extraordinary advancements in the fields of science, medicine, technology, arts, humanity, and every other facet of human life. At the same time, however, it is also an era of utter chaos and destruction where humans have developed the kind of capabilities and habits that could destroy the entire human civilization and the entire planetary life within a blink of an eye. Volumes can be written about the critical issues that the world is facing in current times. In this segment I discuss, although only briefly, a few of these daunting challenges. Without getting too deep into any of these issues, my intent is only to highlight the problem, and use it to build my case for meditation.

2.1.1 - Chaos And Destruction

"If you find yourself in a hole, the first thing you do is stop digging."

-- Will Rogers

Life is challenging, to say the least. If you look around today at the state of your neighbourhood, your community, town, city, country and around the world, all of them tend to signal that something's wrong with the human mind. The appalling conditions of war, poverty, hunger, climate crisis, health crisis, the rise in crime, violence, religious extremism, the population explosion, destruction of natural resources, deforestation, food and water insecurity, the corruption, the greed, the dangerous rise and reach of big tech, and so on, all pointing to an ever-increasing fragmentation of the human mind. Does it not?

We are at our own peril, and the breaking news is that most of the human-manufactured destruction has happened in just the last 150 years, since the dawn of the industrial age.

The human race is causing an irreversible harm to our planet and to planetary life by plundering its resources as if there is no tomorrow. We have polluted the air and oceans with chemicals, pushed many animal and marine species into extinction, and killed the life-sustaining coral reefs. In a short span of a hundred years, we melted the polar ice caps that were stable for millions of years. In the same timeframe, we poked holes in our atmosphere, tore down the Amazon rain forests which act as the lungs of our planet and are home to over fifty percent of animal and plant species.

And then, we have produced enough lethal, chemical, nuclear, and biological weapons to wipe off human civilization overnight. A very scary situation, indeed. In pursuit of peace by way of war, and in the name of human development we are ripping the planet apart. Humans have essentially impacted every habitat in the biosphere.

Phaethon Syndrome[12]

In Greek mythology, Helios, the old Greek god of the sun, once handed his dear son Phaethon the reins of his chariot he used to steer the sun across the sky. It was the toughest job in the galaxy and one which required strength, confidence, fearlessness, and control. Phaethon, lacking these qualities, however, lost his grip on the reins and the sun fell off its assigned orbit, killing Phaethon and roasting the earth below.[12]

Like Phaethon, we find ourselves today with the immense power of governance, technology and warfare- but put them into the wrong hands, and they can push the world into eternal darkness. *We are the victims of our own success.* The same ingenuity that brought progress, prosperity and advancement of humans, can bring chaos and destruction, and our experience here on earth so far certainly seems to bear out this point.

In his book Sapiens, Harari tells us that Homo Sapiens went to Australia, and within a thousand years of their arrival, twenty-five of the biggest mammals that lived there became extinct. Native Tasmanians who survived 10,000 years were exterminated within 100 years of the arrival of Sapiens. Early humans caused mass extinction of plants and animal species wherever they went; North America lost 34 out of 47 species of large mammals and South America lost 50 out of 60.

So even in our less-evolved form we screwed stuff up pretty quickly.[39] We take wondrous things and abuse them to extinction as we have done with our planet, environment, water, air, food, technology…everything.

In his inspirational writings, renowned author C.S. Lewis notes, "Our world is an enemy occupied territory, invaded by powerful evils bent on destroying all that is good. And the problem is us. The crooked and perverse generation the prophets and psalmists spoke about many thousands of years ago is our own...All the notions of modernity and progress and all the advances in technology expertise have not brought an end to war."

This paragraph is sadly still relevant today, and especially so. The modern era has ushered in a different form of warfare – the information war. The nexus of political states, politicians, military apparatus, big tech and rogue actors engage in information hacking, spreading computer virus attacks, crippling critical infrastructure, indulge in unauthorized surveillance, and so on.

China is banning US based technology platforms, and the US and its western allies are banning China based technology. The systems algorithms and some AI based programs are designed to feed on our privacy, and the tech corporations are reaping unimaginable amounts of wealth, and becoming dangerously powerful.

The Webster's Dictionary recently declared its "word of the year 2024" to be "Polarization", meaning division into opposing extremes of groups or interests and factions. Everywhere around the world we see today, our society is more divided than ever.

This division takes many classic forms - race, color, religion, language, political beliefs, economic policies, governance methods, technology acceptance, civil rights, gun control, abortion rights, and so on. The British ruled the entire world with a "divide and rule" policy. The irony is, that very imperial policy is still active in some places in the present times, only the ways and means have changed. The monarchy structures are replaced by democratic and communist forms of government, and technology is leveraged to control and influence.

Furthermore, in an era of internet and social media today it is easy to form and share an opinion about almost everything, but which in turn seems to drive more disagreements about, well, almost everything. New conspiracy theories surface each passing day deceiving millions. There is a rampant spread of fake news and misinformation every passing hour. The generative AI is employed to create and spread fake narratives at a greater scale. And all of this leads to a greater political divide, and greater polarization fuelling more hatred and anger.

The world's religions have not resolved any of the existential problems either. On the contrary, religious extremism has led to rise in hatred, division, the 'Us versus Them' mentality, intolerance and even terrorism. The entire world is running away from the truth. The current state indicates that we are somehow not getting it right. While enjoying the benefits of spectacular economic and technological development, we find ourselves at a tipping point in human evolution. Humanity faces devastating challenges and threatens planetary life itself. These conditions indicate unmistakably that our very existence is at stake.

So, where does this take us as a human race? Are we then willing to heed the warnings that these conditions are sounding about how we live?

Again,

"If you find yourself in the hole,
the first thing you do is stop digging."

-- Will Rogers.

2.1.2 - Age of Consumerism

"A real conquest of space is of the inner space that contains all the worlds. Any conquest of material nature is illusion."

-- Gil Fronsdal

We live in an age where chasing material pleasure seems to be the way of life and this habit is deeply embedded into the modern lifestyle. The modern economies of the world present and promote a model of spending and all of us are running around, gathering creature comforts at a relentless pace. On an everyday basis, we indulge in extraordinary levels of consumption and acquisition of materialistic objects that would eclipse Cleopatra's wildest desires. And even when we have everything we may want and need, we remain depressed and unhappy.

The consumerist ethos that took a firm hold in the 20th century urges us to strive for more. American homes are filled with things. The closets are stuffed with clothes and shoes, most of which see the light once a year. The rooms are stuffed with furniture of all kinds, decor, electronics, and big appliances. Every suburban household garage is stuffed with tools and machines, most of which rarely get used.

The basements are stuffed with storage boxes, gym equipment, gaming equipment, most of which have been sitting there for years gathering dust. There are big houses with less people and more possessions. And then there is some more stuff tucked away in rental storage units because there isn't enough space left in the house.

Furthermore, in order to support our lavish lifestyle-to buy more, eat more, drink more, consume more, to get a bigger house, better car, the latest phone, go on luxury vacations, buy fancy clothes, and so on, we enslave ourselves to banks and corporations and the credit card companies. The credit card companies employ tactics to lure you into buying their products and many end up trapped into a perpetual debt cycle as a result. In 2024 the Americans have a staggering 1.2 trillion dollars in credit card debt, 18 trillion household debt, and 2 trillion student debt. We get buried under the load of massive debt -

home loans, student loans, car loans, personal loans. And nearly every minute of our life revolves around paying bills, writing cheques, paying mortgage, settling credit card debts, paying taxes, paying for insurance and utilities, saving for retirement, paying medical bills - and while doing all this we must still believe that we are living the 'American Dream'.

Just the process of buying things has become incredibly easy. On the wonder-tool in the palm of your hands, with a mere click and flick of a button you can buy literally anything and everything from anywhere in the world, from a hair-pin to a jumbo jet. And there always exists some great offers and discounted deals all year round- fifty percent off, eighty percent off, one day delivery, same day delivery, free delivery, no questions asked return policy, and so on.

In addition, there is no dearth of holiday sales, festive sales, winter sales, New Year sales, and so on. Religious holidays have become shopping festivals. For example, you will have a pre-Christmas sale in October, then a Christmas sale in December, then a post-Christmas sale in January, then an extended Christmas sale in February. Every sale is marketed and advertised by the stores and the brands as a once-in-a-lifetime opportunity.

Deep down, everyone knows that having year-round discounts is a gimmick, and that you are being fooled and that the prices are only being jacked up to be later lowered during a sale. But you still cannot stop yourself from being pulled into the shopping frenzy and grabbing the best deal.

More and more boxes are landing on our doorstep each passing day. The market introduces new buzz words like "Spaving", combining the words spending and saving to mean "spend more to save more." We buy countless products we don't really need and until a few minutes back we didn't know even existed. And despite the buying frenzy we are thirstier for more at the end of the day. Take a moment to pause and imagine the cumulative burden in acquiring, discarding, repairing, maintaining, and safeguarding your possessions.

"Consumerism sees consumption of even more products and services as a positive thing. It encourages people to treat themselves, rather spoil themselves by overconsumption. Indulgence is good and frugality is bad, is the wrong message spread by the commercial entities. The corporations exploit and hijack the science of neurophysiology consciously aimed at the hyperactivation of dopamine and endorphin functions of the brain, pushing mass stimulation and addiction."[43] The consumerism model, while promising satisfaction at every turn, relies on you never being satisfied.

Time Kasser, a renowned psychologist, found in his research that the more people value materialistic aspirations as goals, the lower is their happiness, and the fewer pleasant emotions they experience day to day.[13] Genuine happiness does not come from possessing things, but from a deep sense of contentment. In the era of consumerism and social media, however, we never feel that we have enough.

There is always a bigger and better object of our desire we endlessly chase. And the more you desire the more miserable you will be, because the more you desire the more will be your expectations, and less grateful you will be.[55] We must learn to tone down our materialistic demons, wake up to the madness of buying more "stuff" every day, and really figure out how to live with less.

2.1.3 - Hyper-Individualism and Loneliness

"All happiness in the world stems from wanting others to be happy.

All suffering in the world stems from wanting the self to be happy."[34]

-- Shantideva

Again, without getting into too deep I intend to highlight the existential issue and use it to prepare and present my case on meditation.

We also live in an age of hyper-individualism, isolation, and a degree of self-absorption that'd make Narcissus blush. Modern culture celebrates individuality and promotes self-importance. The worship of the self has become a central preoccupation and we see ourselves as separate from each other. In the backdrop of an ever increasing population, the isolation has also risen exponentially.

The cultural ecology seems to have shifted from "We are in this together and we thrive as a community" to "I am on my own, free to do as I choose". The community culture based on mutual support, sharing, respect for elders, and joint family structures seems to be disappearing and being replaced by a stubbornly individualistic mentality.

There is this overriding drive of "I, Me, Myself" which cannot help manipulating, competing, and exploiting others. This idea of "I" makes us narcissistic and self-centered. The western culture today reflects individualistic mindset, seemingly unwilling to consider how we fit collectively as a whole. The Easterners who proclaimed "Vasudhaiva Kutumbakam", a Sanskrit phrase meaning "The world is one big family", also seem to follow the West in adopting the individualistic way of living in the modern times. Although God made us equal, replicas of the same eternal spirit, we don't feel that way. We harbour the "I versus You" mentality and pursue selfish interests.

The renowned author C.S. Lewis says "We must picture hell as a state where everyone is perpetually concerned about their own desires, advancement, dignity, and selfish goals; where everyone has a grievance, and everyone lives with envy, hatred, self-importance and resentment."

Loneliness

One of the famous hosts on American television shows, Dr Phil, has termed loneliness as new-age epidemic. In his show hosted on Fox channel, he presented some alarming statistics about loneliness. Although these numbers reflect the state of affairs in the United States, there are similar compelling findings across several other countries in the world, sounding an alarm about the spread of loneliness crisis in the modern world.

1. About 35% of Americans over the age of 45 are chronically lonely.[12]
2. The percentage of people expressing feelings of loneliness in 2020 was 71%, up from 53% in 2019.
3. Only 8% of Americans reported to have important conversations with their neighbors in a given year.[12]
4. The loneliness may lead to serious health conditions like heart diseases and shortening of life span by as much as 14%.
5. Over 30% households in America are single person households, suggesting a collapse of marital relationships and family structure.

6. There is a huge financial cost attached to loneliness which makes it a big deal. It costs over 6.7 billion dollars in medical spending and 154 billion dollars to employers annually.

The rising loneliness, not just in the West, but around the world, is a public health crisis. Humans are psychosocial beings and we thrive in an interconnected codependent environment. Modern research shows that loneliness is associated as one of the leading causes with mental health issues and chronic health conditions. "Some international surveys show a rise in loneliness particularly amongst millennials and the minorities."[43]

The dark effects of social isolation and hyper individualism are reflected in extremist mentalities, suicides and mass shootings.[4] There is always a lonely man who fell through the cracks of the society, who lived a life of solitary disappointment and who one day decided to take a blood-drenched revenge on society, leaping from insignificance to infamy.

How do you otherwise explain the Uvalde, Texas shooting of several innocent elementary school children? How do you explain the multiple shooting incidents, big and small, that seem to happen every day of the week across American cities? These acts of violence result not from the sale of guns alone, but mainly from the mental health issues with the mostly-young and lonely perpetrators who are pushed to the brink of insanity.

The loneliness is also found to be the leading cause of depression, suicides, and drug addiction.[12] "Since 1999, suicide rates in the US have risen 30%. Between 2006 and 2021, the suicide rate for age 10-17 rose by 70%. Roughly 4500 Americans kill themselves every year. Add to that thousands more who die from drug overdose every year. The fentanyl overdose killed 70000 Americans in 2022, and the opioid addiction kills, on average, 72000 every year."* Drug and opioid use is one of the wider sets of mass phenomena of the feeling of meaninglessness that results from, among other factors, loneliness, hopelessness, and individualistic mentality.

Jelly Roll, one of the most famous Grammy award winning musicians of recent times in the US, and someone with a history of drug addiction, was invited to a Senate hearing at Washington D.C. on the subject of Mental Health and Addiction. In his opening statement he said "190 people die each day in the US from drug overdose. The Boeing 737 carries the same number of passengers. Imagine what would happen if one plane goes down each day. The world media would be covering it all day long and governments will take immediate action...instead of blaming the addict we must address the root cause behind addiction...."

In a similar context, the former Surgeon General of America, Dr. Vivek Murthy, has declared loneliness, drug use and social media use as an epidemic. In particular, he has issued an evidence-based policy directive on the use of social media by kids which is welcomed by parents, teachers, and the public at large. The next section of the chapter highlights the problem of social media addiction in greater detail.

*Statistics presented on TV show on WVIA and PBS news hour.

2.1.4 - Addiction To Phone and Social Media

Over the past couple of decades with the advancement in digital technology, a new kind of problem has surfaced (creeped, rather) into our lives, which is - our addiction to smartphones and social media. Please note that I am consciously (and cautiously) saying it is the "addiction" which is the problem and not necessarily the technology itself. Being able to connect and communicate with anybody, anytime, in any corner of the world today with such ease is nothing short of a miracle. The blessing, however, can quickly turn into a curse when things get out of control.

We are glued to our phones, and our minds and our attention is being imprisoned by this gadget. We cannot imagine staying away from our phones for more than a few minutes. Just notice how paranoid you get if you ever lose your phone or misplace it somewhere and are unable to find it. The stress response kicks in as if you just spotted a tiger running towards you in the bush. The world comes to a stop and you experience a great sense of shock and depression.

As we move deeper into the digital age, most of us feel left out if we are not literally plugged into something all the time. We live in an always "on" and never "off" culture. And with these pressures it's no wonder that few of us get time to connect with ourselves and be in the present.

Then while using our phones and tablets we are constantly calling, texting, scrolling, posting, commenting, and flipping through apps. There is this constant pull on our minds to stay engaged with the device. This overuse drains our energy, tires our mind, and shrinks our attention span. And with the massive rise in our connections and conversations on social media, our lives are getting noisier than ever before. Clearly, our attachment to our phones and social media, making it the most important object of our lives, is greatly costing us our peace of mind and well-being.

We, and by that I mean quite a lot of us, are glued to our phones and many of us have a constant urge to stay active on social media, be relevant, be present, post, post, post, reply, reply, reply, scroll, scroll, flip, flip, every second, every minute, share pictures, share videos, engage in unproductive discussions, arguments, debates, and comparisons which potentially ruin our peace of mind.

Furthermore, living in the virtual world we have forgotten to look up and engage with real people and the physical world around us. We all know that our in-person conversations are more enriching and full when compared with the behind-the-flatscreen conversations. Its organic. We can feel the energy of the other person present in the room and we tend to connect a lot better.

Teens and young adults spend hours and hours each day behind the screens, online, on social media, phone, TV, Tablets, and gaming consoles. Modern research has shown a direct correlation between the number of hours spent online and a sharp rise in cases of depression, anxiety, and suicides. "Social media can make you feel worse about yourself and increase the feeling of loneliness. It has also contributed to the rise of different addictive disorders, such as gambling, gaming, and compulsive sexual behavior, wreaking havoc in the lives of many families."[67]

Acknowledging the seriousness of this issue Australia has become the first country in the world to enact a law banning social media for kids age 16 and younger. The various other countries are now considering similar enactments to safeguard the younger population from the ill effects of social media and the hazards of online presence.

Researchers also found a direct correlation between the amount of time students spend on their phones, and increasing levels of distraction coupled with a lack of focus on academic activities.[51] Teenagers, and even adults, glued to their phones wait for the next 'ting' and 'ding' and 'tzzz' to alert them that they have been liked or tagged or thought of by someone, in someone's post. What is that doing to their brains and the quality of thoughts and emotions? The brain is in a perpetual mode of waiting for the next alert, and the tings and dings cause high levels of tension and anxiety.

The social media landscape is commanding you to click and sample one thing after another. You cannot afford today to not be on TikTok, FB, IG, WhatsApp, Snapchat, or else you will feel left out and miss all the cool stuff. That's the common yet false mentality of today's time. Some people want to show off how cool their life is, how much fun they are having every day, partying, vacationing, and having a large number of friends and followers.

They see others posting happy photos of their gloriously flashy and successful life and in an effort to not be seen as losers they try to imitate it and fake it. On the inside their life is crumbling, they are feeling miserable, but on the outside they post toothpaste-ad-smile photos like their life is all hunky dory.

And there is so much to consume, share, read, comment, and be bothered about. Flipping through apps and pages, we consume a wide variety of information without really absorbing anything completely. It is synonymous to aimlessly wandering on the streets for no good reason, like window shopping, and which makes it all an unproductive pursuit.

The algorithmic and curated content of the apps keep you hooked up.[39] The social media outlets are masterful at using psychological warfare. Your attention is precious and the whole digital world is competing for it for profit.

The technology companies hire behavioral scientists who recommend adding features to the apps and websites that are addictive in nature. This is the same strategy that the fast-food industry has cunningly used for decades, using the food scientists to curate finger-licking-good addictive happy-meals that millions crave. And then there are marketing scientists who create ads for these companies enhancing their product's desirability. They grab your attention and lock you in with freebies, offers, ease of use, rewards, personalization, and so on.

"Our addiction to gadgets - phones, devices, video games, home entertainment - is feeding on the tendency of the human brain to be scattered, unfocused, controlled by negativity and fear, making us feel worse from comparison, being left out, not being enough, feeling jealous, and not feeling contentment in anything at all. Text messages, emails, video games, social media, TV, all can over-stimulate our pleasure centres and permanently change or damage certain areas of the brain."[26] Just like the term WMD used for the weapons of mass destruction, a new term has emerged in present times, SMD - Social Media driven destruction. The powerful SM platforms enable the spreading of misinformation and conspiracy theories, breeding a lot of fear in the masses. Fear leads to panic, panic leads to pain, pain leads to anger, and anger leads to hate. And this toxic cycle leads to destructive behavior.

Furthermore, we put our trust into smartphones, tablets, and smart home appliances with voice-activated technology capabilities, not really knowing what kind of surveillance and listening features are built into these devices and gadgets. We find ourselves besieged by messages of buying every single day.

Have you ever noticed, for example, you are having a conversation with your family about vacations and you say, "Hey, let's take a vacation to Florida..." And a few minutes later when you check your inbox, there it is, emails about Disney cruises, vacation rentals, Orlando hotels, and so on. The relevant ads also start popping up on your social media screens. The irony of it all is that we have gotten so used to such daily occurrences that it does not scare us to know our privacy is being invaded to this extent.

It's time we check our habits in using mobile phones and social media, and be smart about how much time we spend online and for what purposes. While consuming online feed we must ask - Does it make me feel smarter, inspired, stronger, and happier? Is it teaching me something useful, or modelling something positive, or sharing an experience that I can learn and enjoy? Or does it make me feel that I am out of shape and lazy, or that I'm missing out on all the fun, or it makes me jealous and spiteful towards others, or that I am a terrible person because these posts make me think that way? (Men's Health magazine)

2.1.5 - The Entertainment Trap

Here's another form of addiction that barely gets noticed - the TV entertainment and media we consume. Be it violence or reality TV, promoting the 'anything goes' culture in the name of progressive and liberal mentality, pornography, or the unreal expectations set by social media - it's a silent epidemic that's gradually overwhelming our minds. In this brief segment I highlight the impact of this aspect on human minds, and which I call the toxic-entertainment trap.

The television and streaming media present countless shows that portray the shallowest, crassest and most self-centered values imaginable, and are punctuated by commercials which inflate desires and entice viewers into buying.[13] Besides violence, things like crime, vulgarity, toxicity, extravagance - everything is glorified. Pop culture amplifies the smallest of evils and creates an industry out of it.

A sixty-minute show is punctuated by thirty minutes of commercials that entice viewers into buying things they don't need. With no self-governance or moral guardrails, it's a quicksand we get sucked into without even knowing, ultimately paying the price with our mental well-being.

Let me be clear. I am not against the depiction of sex or violence when necessary. Every form of entertainment has its use. The trouble starts when the human mind fails to moderate. And entertainment companies play on this failing of the mind. The ease of access to porn today is quite unnerving, and younger minds are getting exposed to stuff their juvenile minds are not capable of processing.

Pornography accounts for 20% of all mobile internet searches and 13% of all the web searches[60]. These numbers scream addiction at alarming levels and the habit can potentially cause irreversible damage to the human brain. It is already destroying beautiful marital relationships, destroying families, and causing a rut in the moral and cultural values of the society.

Add to this, the unreal world of social media, where entire lives are projected through lenses and filters that again create unrealistic expectations on young, impressionable minds.

Then, the first thing in the morning, we habitually watch news on TV, then listen to the news on the car radio: all about war, mass shootings, gunmen at school, rape, robbery, violence, pandemic, floods, storms, divisive politics, media propaganda, and so on. And we end our day with some more news before going to bed at night. In a thirty-minute news cycle, everything is sensationalized.

Author Eknath Easwaran says "We eat with our eyes and ears too. If we listen to poisonous negativity, violence, gossip, it is no different than consuming junk food, sugary stuff, fries, saturated fats and we are bound to get sick with fear, paranoia, insecurity, lack of trust, doubt, and other negative feelings."

We need to become aware of the dangers of the toxic-entertainment trap which involves long-term, sometimes life-long, neuroplastic changes in the brain causing irreversible damage.

2.2 - Inner World: The Restless Mind

Let us leave aside for a moment the problems of the outer world, and turn our attention inward and view the problems of our inner world. Just like the outer world, our inner world is riddled with chaos and turmoil of its own kind.

2.2.1 - The Cycle of Past, Future, and Negative Thinking

"Ten thousand flowers in spring
The moon in autumn
A cool breeze in summer
Snow in winter
If your mind is not clouded by unnecessary things
This is the best season of your life."

-- Chinese Wu Men[2]

"Past exists only in Memory, it is not real
Future exists only in Imagination, it is not real
We exist only in the Present, the only real"

We are imprisoned in our minds behind the walls of the past and the future. A moment of self-reflection would make it apparent that we are always either living in the past or in the future, but rarely in the present, in the here and now. Our mind is occupied with the memories of the past that is already rolled up, or with the worries about the future that hasn't been rolled out yet. When occupied with the memories of the past the mind is more often, by virtue of conditioning, caught up in negative emotions attached to the past events.

Some past situations, some past hurts, unconsciously float into our consciousness and like a gunpowder pile set on fire, one thought leads the chain reaction of multiple other thoughts and floods your mind with negative emotions. Looking at some old photos, for example, you spot an old friend who betrayed you, or your ex-wife who cheated on you and broke your trust, say, and this memory sets off a storm of negative feelings like resentment, anger, guilt, shame, disgust, and so on.

[40]Simply by recalling the scene to your mind you will undergo the same reactions and sensations you felt at the time, hypnotically, and reliving the event as though it were actually happening to you, over and over again.[36] We may wish that certain events in the past had never occurred, but feel powerless to move beyond them. What happened in the past is still dictating what exists for us in the present.

When we are not in the past, we are in the future, worrying, anxious, fearful about a lot of things. Our minds are storytelling machines, making predictions, calculating probabilities, imagining the worst, and believing these stories as facts - Will I get the job? Will I get the promotion or will the boss play the racist card and choose one of 'his kind'? Will she say yes when I propose? What if she never talks to me again? Will I ever be successful and rich? Will I ever find true love? Will I ever be popular on social media? Will I ever lose weight? Will I ever be paroled and get to go home to my family? and so on.

Sitting in a parked car with a foot on the gas pedal, not going anywhere, we burn a lot of energy running stories in our minds, mostly worrying, inflating desires, subtly guided by the phantoms of our imaginations.

The more time we spend in the past and future, the more we get stuck in recreating the past and worrying about the future, and thereby allowing trauma and negative thoughts to arise unnoticed into our consciousness causing an emotional drain. This is essentially how we construct our inner prison and entrap ourselves. And a lot of our thinking tends to be negative, running the worst case scenarios in our minds about both the past events and the future events of our life.

Author Daniel Amen terms the negative thinking phenomena as ANTs - Automatic Negative Thoughts, that pop up in your mind uninvited, out of a habituated and conditioned mind, and makes you feel sad, worried or upset. He notes, "The ANTs generate feelings of helplessness, hopelessness, anger, guilt, bitterness, and others, which are cognitively, emotionally, rationally, and spiritually destructive."

"The suffering follows a negative thought
as wheels follow oxen that draw it
The happiness follows a positive thought
as a shadow that never leaves."

--Gautama Buddha

We injure ourselves with negative thinking. We hold old hurts and never get over them. Instead of releasing pain through letting go and forgiveness, we release it into our minds, clam up, internalize the anger, and eventually explode in unhealthy ways. No matter how sophisticated our minds are made, the fact remains that their basic contents - thoughts, feelings, beliefs, reasoning - powerfully affect our bodies, for better or for worse. Apparently, man is the only animal capable of making himself sick with negative thinking.[37]

In his book 'Mind to Matter' the author Dawson Church notes, "Negative thinking drives up cortisol (one of our primary stress hormones, fight or flight) even when there is no tiger in the grass. Our brains ruminate on the bad things that happened in the past or the bad things that might happen in the future. Even if it never happened and will never happen, we can nonetheless focus on it, contemplate it, imagine it, talk about it, and catastrophize about it." We keep repeating the same stressful thoughts over and over again, and our mind becomes like a broken record.

This all means that as long as our consciousness is trapped in the dungeons of the past and future, no meaningful change can take place in our lives. We need to take the needle off the broken record and let go.

Marlo Morgan, author of 'Mutant down Under' makes a very interesting point in this regard in her book. She says, "When the mind is filled with negative feelings of the past, then people are non-living. Breathing does not mean being alive. It just tells you whether the body is ready for burial or not. Not all breathing people are in the state of aliveness and vibrancy and fullness."

We walk through our daily lives seemingly unaware, locked into a past-future state of living and habitual thinking patterns, which looks more like we are sleepwalking. Externally your life is new, but internally you are experiencing the same mental reactions, the same psychological tendencies. This short story of the "sleepwalker family" beautifully sums up our current state of existence. Everyone in this family walks in sleep. At night each one sleep-walks to the kitchen, opens the fridge, grabs a bite of pizza, pasta and drinks, and goes back to sleep.

In the morning nobody could explain why the fridge was empty.

We are the victims of Hijacked awareness. The endless cycle of past and future thinking is part of the basic nature of the human mind, but that doesn't mean you are doomed forever. We must wake up to the price we are paying by being stuck in the cycle.[5] The mind, the ego, likes the past because the past is familiar and safe. But look at what it is costing you! Take note of behavioural patterns that show up repeatedly in your life. Examine your own narrative and how your own thinking affects your emotions.

Ram Dass, author of 'Better Here Now', says, "A lot of suffering is self -induced. We dwell in the past and worry about the future instead of existing as fully as possible in the present." He urges us to go from 'ego-awareness' (where one is prey to memories, anxiety, judgment) to 'soul-awareness' (a meditative state where we are calm and unburdened).

A beautiful example of a true awakening and of finding freedom from the entrapment of the past is reflected in Edith Edger's courageous story. At age 16, Edith Eger (a Hungarian Jewish and an internationally acclaimed author) and her family were sent to gas chambers at Auschwitz.[12] She miraculously survived and later on wrote in her memoir, "It is too easy to make a prison out of pain, out of our past. As long as I was holding Hitler in chains and exerting my emotional energy, I was in chains with him, locked in a damning past, locked in grief. So, I forgave him and freed myself."

Edith Eger was able to examine and recognize the part of her past that imprisoned her mind and therefore her well-being, and this awareness became the pathway to her awakening. What a beautiful freedom, indeed.

2.2.2 - Monkey-mind, Bondage, And Stress

"You are never more powerless than you are when you are immersed in a whirlpool of thoughts."

-- Roy Masters

The 'Monkey Mind' is a term coined by Buddha himself way back in the 6th century BC, but it applies today more than ever. It compares the human mind with its incessant thinking to a monkey that jumps from one branch to another, from one tree to another. The monkey swinging through the trees grasps one branch and lets it go, only to seize another, and then another.

Similarly, the human mind is restlessly swinging from one thought to another, and then another. We tend to over-complicate and over-think things. Research suggests that humans think on an average 50,000 to 70,000 thoughts in a day, and most of which are repetitive and negative. Due to this incessant noise and in presence of the other stressors of everyday life, the mind is always working in an overloaded state.[40]

In his book, Beyond The Unknown, author Roy Masters notes "Becoming lost in the machinery of your thinking makes you vulnerable to emotional stress from two directions. First, you start reacting with frustration, resentment, and fear to the mistakes you find yourself making day to day; and secondly, you find yourself overreacting to memories of the past, mistakes that keep coming back to haunt you. Your thinking makes you feel and your feelings make you think; around and around you go in a squirrel cage of anger, anxiety, stress and confusion."

In this context it is worthwhile to note that according to the ancient Vedic philosophy our thoughts are the very source of our Karma, and from our thoughts flows everything: our words, actions, desires, situations, circumstances, experiences, and destiny.

A short story of an old man and his son beautifully illustrates the constant rise and fall of emotions in the human mind. This old man lives in a village with his son whom he loves dearly. One day he gifts his son a pony and watching him ride the pony with excitement makes the old man *happy*. A week later the pony runs away, the son is crying, and this makes the old man *sad* and *depressed*. A few days later the pony returns with a stallion. The son is joyous, happy, and excited, and seeing him that way makes the old man *happy*.

Then one day while riding the stallion son falls off its back and breaks his leg. This makes the old man *sad* and *worried*. The doctor is called who puts a cast on the son's broken leg and he is able to walk again with crutches. This makes the old man *happy*. A week later war is declared in the region and all young men are mandated to enroll. This makes the old man *sad*. Seeing him in a cast the king's men refused to enroll the old man's son. This makes the old man *happy*.

This is, in a way, our own story. We are perpetually caught up in the cycle of happiness and sadness, positive and negative emotions, not only due to the way we perceive a situation, but also because of our attachments. The story highlights the fact that anything which we are attached to can bring happiness in one instance and suffering in the next - a central lesson in

Buddhism. Our never-ending desires bundled with our bondage to people, things, money, car, house, clothes, sneakers, food, sex, and so on, becomes the very source of our misery.

Misery comes out of our attachments. Our clinging creates misery.[56] We cling to that which we have and we constantly desire that which we don't have, and in between the two we are crushed. We must become aware of how our desires and attachments create so much tension in our lives on a daily basis, and begin to train our minds in a way that lessens this burden.

Furthermore, life is always filled with ups and downs. You encounter an unforeseen circumstance, a challenging situation, such as an accident, a death of a loved one, life-threatening illness, a loss of a certain kind, or a shocking discovery of some sort, then you will instantly be stressed out - all the above come without warning.[13] And since we are already burdened by the anxieties of day-to-day life beyond our control, such as family responsibilities, relationship issues, job problems, money problems, and so on, an unexpected event creates tension in the body and if poorly managed, send us spiralling down into a pile of smouldering emotional wreckage.

When the mind is working in an overloaded state, we are only existing rather than thriving and living a full vibrant life. The stress on the mind causes stress on the body. A Harvard research study found that emotional stresses are inseparable from the physical states of our bodies, in both illness and health.[45]

The medical literature suggests that chronic stress conditions can make us anxious or depressed, suppress immunity, promote inflammation, narrow blood vessels (promoting vascular diseases throughout the body), encourage cancerous growth, thin the bones, elevate the risk of cardiovascular problems, impair essential cognitive and emotional circuits in the brain, distort hormonal apparatus, accelerate aging, and so on.

Therefore, reducing stress wherever possible, attending to emotions, suspending self-judgements, and taking care of our psychic well-being can have a profound effect on our physical health.

Furthermore, we live in a modern world where speed is worshipped and everything seems to be moving at a rapid pace. We eat in a hurry, drive in a hurry, work in a hurry, talk in a hurry, text in a hurry, do everything in a hurry as if there is a ticking time bomb waiting to go off. We are here, but we want to be there, somewhere else. We are doing this, but we want to do that, something else. We have forgotten how to be sit still, slow down, and soak in the present moment fully. Our calendars are full, and we are multitasking and rushing most of the time. This multitasking scenario might sound familiar—you are watching TV, while eating your meal, while scrolling through apps on our phone, while typing a quick message, while talking to a colleague or friend on video call, while petting your dog on the couch, and while glancing at game scores on other tablet.

You have forgotten to really fully absorb and immerse yourself into a singular experience. You are not paying full attention to anyone or anything because your mind is constantly distracted. And this daily habit has can have a far reaching impact on your quality of life and inner well-being. In today's fast-paced world, without stillness and mindfulness you will miss out on the beauty of life. Think about it.

In summary, unless your mind is unburdened of stress and tension, life in the present will be off balance. Unless you are able to connect deeply with the present moment it'd be hard to find lasting peace and happiness that you seek. For that to happen the number of thoughts you think must go down. It is only in the state of thoughtlessness, really, where life's problems dissolve into the present moment. And one way to achieve that state is through mindful living and practicing meditation.

2.2.3.- The Horses and the Rider: A Zen Story

"You have no better friend than a trained mind. You have no worse enemy than an untrained mind."

-- Buddha

In Eastern tradition, there is a story of a King (you, your spirit, your soul) riding his Chariot (your body) which is drawn by five Horses (your senses) handled by a Driver (your intellect) using the Reins (your mind) to control the Horses.

The Horses are running wild through the streets, pulling the King's chariot. They are running directionless, going left, going right, going straight, turning here, turning there, slowing down then moving fast, running after something, but not really sure which way to go and what to do. The Reins appear to be weak, the Driver appears to have lost control, and the King appears to be sleeping unaware.

A passerby on the street is watching this unfold and shouts out to the King, "Hey sir, where are you going?" The King replies, "I don't know, ask the Driver." The passerby shouts again, "Hey Driver, where are you going?" The Driver replies, "I don't know, ask the Horses."

This is our story. The story of our mind which is held captive by the pull of the senses, perceptions and desires, and driven by an incessant influx of thoughts. We are dragged and pushed and pulled by each sense impression and each thought, going left, going right, going up, going down, in perpetuity. Due to this energy drain the mind is confused, the intellect is unable to make the right decisions, loses control, and the Self remains unaware.

As long as horses are running the show in absence of awareness the Chariot and the King are at a great risk of losing control and ending up in pile of wreckage. Most people who have tried would probably agree that training the mind and bringing it under voluntary control is one of the most difficult tasks a person can undertake.[54] The senses go running after the pleasure and the pull of desire, and trap you into perpetual motion. This story beautifully sums up the state of our conditioned mind which is out of control and driven by desires, senses, pleasures, and negative thinking.

The "conditioned mind" means the programmed mind that has been fed tremendous amount of information right from the moment you are born, giving it a unique identity about who you are, what your religion is, what your culture is, what your language is, what the world is supposed to be like, and so on. You are fed opinions, facts, perspectives, doctrines, theories, prejudices, and traditions. You go to schools and colleges, learning more facts about nature, history, science, and so on.

The data from the outside world is collected by your five senses and stored and processed in your brain. You are literally bombarded with sense stimuli every instant. And over time this enormous volume of sense impressions begin to a certain distinctive pattern within you.

We ourselves built this inner prison of conditioned mind, erected high walls, and locked ourselves inside. You are the builder, but you have now imprisoned yourself in your own home. You have become your own jailor. The conditioning is the vast volume of our Ego, bundled up in our thoughts, beliefs, expectations, memories, fears, habits, biases, values, attitudes and emotional history. We see the universe through the windows of our ego room and most people cannot escape the ego room in a lifetime.

The retaining walls of the mind are nothing more than the strongly agreed-upon and longstanding belief system we hold, consisting of social, cultural and familial conditioning, which together form beliefs about the world.[55] What gets built in the process is a hardened personality and inflated ego.

The story of the Horse and Rider highlights the fact that chasing sensory pleasures is like chasing a mirage. It may be attractive to pursue, but every time we see it, smell it, feel it, taste it, or hear it, we remain thirstier than we were before. This illusion in Indian philosophy is termed as "Maya", which literally means - that which is not.[10] We forget the citadel within us and go running around a desert in search of the shimmering promises that lead us farther and farther away from home.

The story is summed up in this way --

I crave sweets - The Horses (senses) crave sweets, not you.
I am stressed out - The Reins (mind) is weak, not you.
I am emotionally hurt - The Driver (ego) is hurt, not you.
I am tired - The Chariot (body) is low energy, not you.
You have forgotten who you really are - the master of your mind, the King.

When your consciousness is not centered within, it becomes totally focused on the objects of consciousness - the outer world objects absorbed through sense perceptions, and the inner world objects like thoughts, emotions and memory. In meditation, however, by becoming aware of your breath, using it as an anchor, you can deepen your consciousness and achieve the stillness of your mind. And hence the Buddha said, "You have no better friend than a trained mind, and no worse enemy than an untrained mind." The moral of the story is that instead of being an actor at the pull and mercy of your senses and conditioned mind, you become a skilled director of your life.

2.3 - Arriving At Meditation

"To a mind that is still, the whole universe surrenders."[59]
- Lao Tzu
"Seeking happiness outside of ourselves
is like waiting for sunlight in a cave facing north."

--A Tibetan saying

One of the greatest survival stories in recent history is about Ernest Shackleton's 1914 trans-Antarctic expedition aboard the ship named Endurance. A 120-day exploration journey was disastrously converted into a 634-day survival effort when the ship was trapped in polar ice and crushed to pieces. The stranded crew of 27 explorers faced hellish conditions of bitter cold, ice, shortage of food and supplies, mutiny, and much more. However, it was ultimately because of Shackleton's extraordinary leadership and wisdom that the entire crew survived and reached home safely.

Importantly, however, this expedition began with an advertisement in the London papers-[42] men wanted for a hazardous journey, small wages, bitter cold, long months of complete darkness, constant danger, safe return doubtful; honour and recognition in case of success. Who in the world would volunteer for this journey? Amazingly, thousands came forward.

The current state or our world, both the inner and the outer which I presented in the preceding segment, inarguably suggests that we humans embark on a similar expedition in our daily lives and face existential crisis. We know that our actions are hazardous for our world, both inner and outer, but we still insist on selfishly going forward, satisfying our agendas at any cost, risking our mental health, our physical health, and harming the planet.

[42]Sir Edmund Hillary, the first person to climb Mount Everest and to cross Antarctica successfully wrote, "When disaster strikes and all hope is gone, get down on your knees and pray for Shackleton."

The problems of the outer world and the inner world scream existential crisis for humanity and human psyche. For our civilization to right itself and chart a course toward sustainability and prosperity, we must find our proverbial Shackleton to ensure our survival. "There is nothing progressive about being pig-headed and refusing to admit a mistake", says author C.S. Lewis. "If you look at the present state of the world, it is pretty plain that humanity has been making some big blunders. We are on the wrong road. We must wake up to what is happening to us and around us."

Wouldn't an advanced stage of human development suggest that we know how to address our inner and outer world problems, and flourish with peace, joy, happiness, progress and compassion? How do we stay afloat amidst the chaos and complexities of life? And how do we face life's challenges without breaking?

As for the answers to these questions, I am not concerned as to what the governments and countries around the world would do or should be doing, like policies, programs, technology and initiatives of various kinds, to address the various problems faced by humanity. That part is in the outer universe, outside the scope and discussion of this book.

I am, instead, concerned about our inner universe and solving the problems in the inner space which would then flow into the outer universe as we saw in chapter 1, where I covered the concept of the two worlds. This inquiry into finding different ways to resolve the inner conflict brings us at the doorstep of meditation.

There is a Sanskrit verse "Mana Eva Manusyanam Karanam Bandha Moksayoh" (pronounced Ma+Na Ava Man+oos+yaa+nam Car+a+num Bun+the Mok+se+yoho) meaning "As the mind, so the person. Bondage and liberation are in your mind." The entire world is your projection, and meditation is about changing the inner world. It is about self-reformation, self-control, self-adjustment and self-awareness, which is exactly the kind of solution we need to strengthen our inner world.

We are at a critical juncture, a tipping point in the history of the world and facing existential problems. Nothing is more vital than learning to face turmoil with great confidence and awareness, shredding all fears and doubts. I believe that what we need, now more than ever, is inner wisdom, a revolution in our consciousness to shape the trajectory of our life, and more importantly to reclaim our mind's freedom.

The greatest revolution of our generation is
the discovery that human beings, by changing
the inner attitudes of their minds, can
change the outer aspects of their lives

- William James

Meditation is about coming back to experience our present state, fully, again and again. It is about cultivating awareness and living everyday life with mindfulness. Developing the inner strength by practicing meditation will help you break free from the mind's prison which holds you captive into conditioned behaviour, monkey-mind thinking, and the past-future cycle.

In the next chapter I provide an expansive set of definitions of meditation and meditation practice, covering diverse perspectives, and explaining what it really means. For now, it will suffice to know that meditation practice is a powerful vehicle for realizing inner stillness.

A quick caution. Meditation is not a panacea to all the world's problems (including those which I highlighted in the earlier segment). By no means do I intend to suggest as such in any shape or form, and my words must not be misconstrued. My attempt is to establish the connection between the state of the world we live in and the human mind, and how the two worlds influence each other due to the inherent interdependence and interconnectedness.

Human beings also exist in relation to each other. All of us are radiating awareness out into the world and bringing its reflection back to us. If your awareness contains violence, fear, and anger, you will meet these negative qualities out there.

"The real enemy is not outside of us, It is to be confronted within us."

For the mind to become steady and calm, and for you to be able to cultivate awareness and concentration, you must first, as a prerequisite, be able to stop your thinking process and the number of thoughts must go down significantly. The speed of the ever-swinging monkey-mind must be controlled and slowly brought to a standstill. And there are multiple pathways to do it. However, the simplest, most efficient, most traditional and most scientific pathway is the way of breathing-meditation.

There is a switch-off button to your monkey-mind. There is a dimmer button to your restless mind.[5] And this button is your breath. And the process and the mechanism of using your breath to control what goes on in your mind is what meditation (Pranayama) is mainly about in its most traditional sense. I elaborate upon this aspect in Section 3.4.4, explaining in detail the proper way of breathing in meditation, also known as yogic-breathing. The yoga master B.K.S. Iyengar says, "Ignoring the use and development of breath (meditation) is like having a fortune locked in a bank account you forgot the password to."[5]

Generally speaking, however, holistic wellbeing and holistic progress is achieved not by just one particular thing or action in isolation, but by multiple things and actions coming together in harmony and balance. It is brought about by the integration of various practices and pathways of human development including physical exercise, yoga, healthy eating, daily hygiene, moral behaviour, education, building character, developing faith, cultivating awareness, nourishing mindfulness, and in these modern times, mainly by slowing down a little.

A 'wholistic' and a well-rounded approach like such is nothing but "Integral Yoga" and "Yoga of Synthesis" as termed by Sri Swami Satchidananda. It does not simply advocate meditation, but takes into consideration the entire life of a person.[52] The result of integral yoga is – a calm, clear, well-disciplined mind, a sharp intellect, a will that is strong and yet pliable, a heart full of love and compassion, an ego as pure as crystal, and a life filled with supreme peace and joy. A true mental, physical and spiritual harmony.

2.4 - Benefits of Practicing Meditation

I purposefully keep this segment short by providing a snapshot of some of the main benefits of meditation practice, in a simple list format. I recommend you browse through the list slowly and carefully, taking a good mental note of each and every benefit, one by one. These benefits are real and experienced by hundreds of millions of meditation practitioners around the world.

These benefits are also scientifically proven via research studies, the details of which I cover in the next section. More importantly, you can personally achieve all of these benefits simply by choosing to practice meditation daily, for just twelve minutes every day (see innovative and practical "SoZo Meditation" technique in chapters 4 and 7). Bear in mind this list is only the tip of the iceberg of similar compelling benefits and I encourage my readers to do their own research.

The Amazing Benefits of Meditation

1. Lowers stress and anxiety.
2. Lowers depression.
3. Increases happiness and joy.
4. Increases feelings of peace and calm.
5. Increases feelings of well-being.
6. Quieter and sharper mind.
7. Improves focus and concentration.
8. Lowers fear and nervousness.
9. Improves emotion control.
10. Lowers anger and frustration.
11. Improves acceptance and letting go.
12. Improves self-awareness.
13. Increases self-esteem.

14. Better relationships.
15. Boosts social connectedness
16. Improves mental health.
17. Improves brain and cognitive functions.
18. Enhanced memory.
19. Healthier brain circuitry.
20. Reduces symptoms of PTSD.
21. Improves physical health.
22. Reduces hypertension.
23. Better immunity.
24. Reduces inflammation.
25. Reduces risk of cardiovascular diseases.
26. Increases energy and vitality.
27. Slows down ageing.
28. Better quality sleep.
29. Improves spiritual health.
30. Spiritual enlightenment

Just imagine for a moment what your life will be like if you are able to experience even only a few of these benefits. You will feel like a different person altogether who is lighter, happier, calmer, wiser and more in control of his or her emotions. Your life will suddenly blossom like a beautiful flower in the spring and it will shine with the light of a thousand suns. With greater awareness you will feel you have better control over your life and be able to connect deeply with people and the world around you.

Again, these benefits are real. This is not a made-up list. These benefits are backed by science, and experienced by millions in the East as well as in the West in a universal way.

If this does not excite you, I am not sure what would!

Ramana Maharishi, a sage from ancient India, was once questioned by a student, "Master, would meditation answer all my questions?" The Master replied, "No. But it will destroy the questioner." In meditation, your consciousness deepens, your awareness expands, and with that comes greater clarity and infinite wisdom. In that state you connect with your inner Self which is separate from your ego-self that is asking questions.

The ego-self (questioner) starts to disappear and you will see creative answers to life's many questions with ease, leading you into pure awareness and towards an enlightened mind. This also means that meditation-practice will free your Self from mind's captivity as you dis-identify yourself from your ego, emotions, thoughts, memories, and your body.

2.5 - Scientific Research on Meditation

"Unless we can measure something, science won't concede it exists, which is why science refuses to deal with such 'non-things' as emotions, the mind, the soul, or spirit..."

-- Candice Pert, Ph.D., Molecules of Emotion

When talking about meditation and related subjects with the Western audience, I often encounter some degree of hesitation and resistance from some of the folks. This reaction is rooted in their strongly (and often wrongly) held beliefs about meditation, that meditation is either a deeply religious activity linked with Hinduism and Buddhism, or it is a vague spiritual pursuit for achieving enlightenment and merging with the cosmos.

Some even go at length to label it as a mix of mysticism, psychological illusion, even as a black-magic phenomenon. Meditation and its potential role in health and healing is often misunderstood because of its association with mystical eastern traditions.

The misconception arises because many of the sceptics are not aware that the meditation-practice is scientific, and that there is a whole lot of scientific research conducted all around the world which confirms the wide-ranging benefits of meditation. And the West won't bite the meditation pill unless some scientific evidence is presented along with some proven outcomes.

With the hope that it would dispel some of the preeminent myths and clear all the doubts in a sceptical mind, I present here the scientific evidence on meditation, which validates its many benefits for mental health and physical health. You will see how science is now showing us objectively what the yogis have known subjectively for thousands of years.

Meditation has been practiced in the East by Asian and Indian cultures for thousands of years. "By the turn of the 19th century such international movements as the theosophical society were disseminating information about eastern contemplative practices to western public eager for alternate spiritual practices. In 1893 Swami Vivekananda of The Ramakrishna Vedanta order in India began teaching meditation to the audiences at World Parliament of Religions, held in Chicago. These efforts were continued into the 20th century by the likes of Paramahansa Yogananda, Jiddu Krishnamurti, and many others."[52]

However, the scientific studies on meditation started sometime in early 60s at the behest of 'Maharishi Mahesh Yogi', the founder of 'Transcendental Meditation' (TM). It was upon his suggestion, notes Deepak Chopra, that the scientific research studies began in the US and Europe.[2] A concept that the effects of meditation can be measured and validated by means of a scientific experiment in a lab was a novel idea in those times.

It would also prove that you don't have to be of an Indian or Chinese origin to practice meditation, and that the benefits can be experienced by everyone in a universal and scientific and secular way. It was this initiative perhaps that turned out to be the cornerstone of a multi-billion-dollar meditation industry today.

The research beginnings are also credited to Dr. Herbert Benson, a Harvard cardiologist, who flew to the Himalayas in the 1980s, recruited a few Buddhist monks, hooked them up with sensors, and asked them to practice meditation. Based on his research findings he further developed the modern relaxation techniques which are practiced by millions all over the world.

Since the sixties, there have been thousands of scientific studies conducted all over the world in the field of meditation and meditation practices. A quick online search will confirm that a lot of this research also comes from the world-renowned education centres like Harvard, Stanford, Murdoch, Cambridge, Oxford, Johns Hopkins, Penn State, NYU, University of Chicago, and many more.

These studies conducted on different types and forms of meditation practices, and a variety of meditation subjects - from the East and West, old and young, believers and nonbelievers, beginners and experts-have provided empirical evidence proving the wide-ranging effects and benefits of meditation practice.

After monitoring subjects practicing meditation for various physical and mental health parameters such as brain activity, brain scans, heartbeat, pulse rate, blood pressure, glucose levels, respiration rate, oxygen consumption, muscle tension, chemicals, hormones, and various other bodily signs the Western scientists soon agreed upon the positive effects of meditation practice on behavior, physiology, and psychology.

A clear picture is emerging as modern research confirms traditional wisdom. Science has started to reveal to what degree breathing and meditation can enhance well-being.[39] The use of medical technologies like MRI, EEG, PET scans for scanning the brain, has shed a new light on the workings of the human brain and the nature of the human mind. In some studies participants were placed inside MRI machines to measure the volume of each part of the brain before and after meditation. The review found increases in the volume of brain regions (meaning neural growth) involved in - attention control, emotional regulation, and self-awareness.[55]

Many influential studies examined the brain wave patterns of meditators and compared their brain function in normal state of consciousness and in meditation. There are 5 basic brain waves that are picked up by a modern EEG.

Gamma 40-100 Hz, associated with learning

Beta 12-40 Hz, monkey mind, problem solving

Alpha 8-12 Hz, associated with alertness

Theta 4-8 Hz, associated with light sleep

Delta 0-4 Hz, associated with deep sleep

And the most common outcome across various experiments was that of low beta and high delta, indicative that the meditator is in a state of grand awareness, intuition, creativity, and restfulness. By monitoring the functions and activity across various parts of the brain of the meditation subjects, the scientists have established a direct correlation between meditation and improvement in cognitive functions, memory function, reduction in stress, anxiety and depression, and overall emotional well-being. [52]Meditation practice is scientifically proven to be a body-mind (psychosomatic) process characterized by significant physical changes, such as low blood pressure, a decreased heart rate, increased body temperature, and a general sense of intense calm.

I include below a small set of research findings drawn from various references included in the book. A simple google search on the 'scientific research and benefits of meditation' will provide you with similar compelling findings, and I encourage my readers to conduct their own research. Bear in mind the list provided below is only the tip of the iceberg.

a. Research suggests that most forms of meditation will exercise your brain and improve the brain's working memory, memory recall, and maintain cognitive health.[1]
b. Studies have shown that meditation practice improves attention, reduces depression and anxiety, decreases sleepiness, and protects the brain from cognitive decline associated with natural aging. Meditation has also been found to help with weight loss.[59]
c. Research done in 2007 in school students simply using deep breathing techniques, decreased anxiety, nervousness, self-doubt, concentration loss, and improved attendance.
d. More than 70 independent studies conducted at Harvard medical school, Columbia college of physicians and surgeons, and other institutes, found Sudarshan Kriya (a specific form of breathing meditation) was highly effective in treatment of a range of ailments, from chronic stress to joint pain and autoimmune diseases.[65]
e. Meditation practice permanently strengthens neural functioning in specific parts of the brain that are involved with lowering anxiety and depression, enhancing social awareness and empathy, and improving cognitive intellectual functioning.[1]
f. FMRI scans studies at a psychiatric neuroimaging research program at Massachusetts General Hospital, showed that meditation enhances the brain thickness

and neuroplasticity; normally as we age the cerebral cortex thins.[1]

g. 65% increase in dopamine was found when individuals practise yoga nidra, a form of relaxation technique described in chapter 6. Dopamine heightens sensory images, generates pleasurable experiences, stimulates positive thoughts, increases your sense of well-being and allows you to feel safe in the world.

h. The neural circuits activated by meditation buffer you from deleterious effects of aging and stress and give you better control over your emotions. At the very least, such practices help you remain calm, serene, peaceful, and alert. And for nearly everyone it gives you a positive and optimistic outlook in life.[1]

i. Research suggests that meditation consistently takes the practitioner into deeper states of consciousness when compared to everyday consciousness; the brain during meditation is operating in an unusual way. And since the underlying mechanics of meditation are theologically neutral, it can be integrated with any religious doctrines or creed or schools to improve social cooperation and cognitive performance.[1]

j. Meditation reduces stress by approximately 45 percent in some of the most stressed people on the planet - third year medical students who are subjected to regular academic stress.

k. Improvements in many medical conditions, including Hypertension, Cardiac Arrhythmia, chronic pain, insomnia, infertility, recovery from side effects of cancer treatments, and so on.

l. More than seventy independent studies conducted at Harvard mAndy, specifically of Sudarshan Kriya developed by Sri Sri Ravishanankar, was highly effective in treatment of a range of ailments, everything from chronic stress to joint pain and autoimmune diseases.[65]

CHAPTER 3
DEEPER INSIGHTS INTO WHAT MEDITATION IS REALLY ABOUT

3.1 - Clear The Confusion And Debunk The Myths

"Anything can be accepted as truth today, as long as it isn't the truth."[2]

- Deepak Chopra

When you think of mediation, you probably picture a guy, rarely a gal, sitting in the cross-legged posture on the banks of a river, in a serene setting, under a waterfall perhaps, or by a mountain, in a cave, or under a tree perhaps, a sage-like figure in white robes, long beard, a monk in saffron, eyes closed, deep in contemplation, chanting OM and having an air of tranquility around him.

This all looks pretty cool and mystical, and sounds amazing- however, what is he really doing? How could someone, you may wonder, sit comfortably in that posture for hours without getting twitches and pain? And hey, is it not boring to be sitting and doing nothing? Is it easy or is it hard? Why would anybody want to do it? Can I do it? Should I? What is the meaning of it all?

I will provide all the answers shortly. But first, let me address the common myths and misconceptions attached to the practice of meditation, those which inadvertently result in confusion and skepticism. Clearing these doubts will help one understand what the meditation practice is really all about.

Most people have some fanciful and vague ideas about meditation. In that, many consider meditation to be a spiritual or religious pursuit for the people in the East, and something practiced only by Buddhist monks and Hindu saints. Many consider it to be an exotic and mystical practice to achieve an altered state of consciousness. Some call it a new-age fad. Practicing meditation has become increasingly mainstream in the past decade or so with literally every health and fitness centre offering some or the other type of meditation program. The offerings have simply mushroomed in thousands of varieties all over the world. The celebrities are endorsing it by a ton and the social media is spreading its popularity, giving meditation practice a contemporary edge.

What often gives rise to confusion, however, is the too much (of wrong) information, too many perspectives, too many opinions and too many varieties of offerings. A lot of people, especially in the West, equate meditation with the Buddhist mindfulness meditation practices which are popularized in the western world by commercial entities and the media. Painting such an incomplete and incorrect picture of meditation keeps millions from seeking and pursuing meditation-practice.

As a small experiment, say, if you inquire about the meditation programs offered within a 5-mile radius from your residence, at your local area gyms and meditation centres, you will end up, I am sure, being offered a multitude of variety of fanciful practices, all different from each other and which might cost you a fortune. This has been my personal experience. I went to several different training centres to learn meditation and yoga, enrolled in different programs, at different times, with different teachers, learning different techniques, and at the end I found myself back to square one. As a beginner I could not find success with the mindfulness meditation and focused-attention forms, especially those that were over thirty minutes or longer in duration.

People often comment to me that they are simply unsure of which form and type of meditation practice is best for them, that they are confused, and until they can figure it out they feel safer not doing anything. The confusion arises mainly due to the multitude of forms and types of meditation practices available in the marketplace, that range from simple to complex and from spiritual to completely secular. The range of specific techniques is broad and there are several major categories or classes of practices. These myriad styles may include Eastern meditation-practices based on focused attention, open monitoring, loving kindness, insight and concentration, awareness training, Vipassana, and other transcendental meditation forms and types.

Author Loch Kelly explains in his book-The Way Of Effortless Mindfulness, "The focused attention is like looking down from a tower into a river of your breath or on some other object, and intensely focusing upon the object. Open monitoring is like looking from the open sky to thoughts, feelings, sensations as separate objects like clouds, birds, coming in and out of your awareness."[29] The Vipassana meditation is about seeing things as they are, using speechless contemplation and letting go, while the TM (transcendental meditation) represents the teachings of Maharishi Mahesh Yogi and is based on effortless Mantra yoga. Furthermore, in advanced stages, and this is not really the main purpose of meditation for an ordinary practitioner, the intense practice might focus upon a variety of esoteric goals like developing forgiveness, enhancing sensuality, dissolving the self, merging with the cosmos, expanding consciousness, and becoming one with God.[1]

Meditation originated in ancient India's philosophical systems five thousand years ago, and from those origins the foundational practices have evolved into various different forms and types spread across Asia into Buddhist traditions, and into the Western world in the late twentieth century. It is important we understand that mindfulness meditation is but one aspect the West took from the East, and many commercial entities have repackaged these practices for Western consumption. A lot of these practices originally designed for monks and monastery lifestyles are customized and marketed to ordinary men and women of the modern world, like us, who do not have the same level of understanding and awareness as that of a monk. Neither do we have the same level of patience, discipline, intent, and the right environment as that of a monk. And which is simply the reason why, these practices tend to be not as successful with most of us.

The kind of practices that require focusing and monitoring and labelling makes our mind work harder when the point is to relax the mind. They exert more stress on the mind when the whole purpose of meditation is to lower the mental activity. Author Rajshree Patel notes, "We are asking a mind that is already unfocused, judgmental, restless, caught up in the cycle of past and future, to be a wise and compassionate Buddha. If the Yogis (meditators) of the past and Buddha himself could hear the way we talk about meditation today, I think they'd have a big belly laugh,"[5] or perhaps a sense of great shock. Personally, it took me took me some time to realize that not every offering is fit for you. It is, in a way, the same principle that exists for the physical workout. Not every form and type of physical exercise is fit for you. You need to know what works best for you and what you really need. Many people leap into intensive practices without realizing the adverse effects on your mind and body from following the wrong approach. And so you must always be mindful of your choices.

Let me be very clear, there is no competition between the traditional Indian meditation practices and Buddhist mindfulness forms, or between the mindfulness practices and

Vipassana, or between Vipassana and other modern offerings in the market. Each one is a different path, I believe, in its own right, leading to a common destination- towards healing, peace, restfulness, and ultimately into the realm within. You must examine the various types from the point of view of how they simply mean to deepen your consciousness and free you from mind's captivity. These various paths and practices, the choice, is synonymous to the choice we have about the different modes and models of transportation used to arrive at a common destination. You may prefer a bike over a car, a train over a bus, a boat over a plane, or a BMW over a Mercedes, a sedan over a SUV, and so on. At the end of the day, it is about what works best for you. It is about what resonates with you the most and is consistent with your personal, ethical, and spiritual beliefs.

So as to gain a full and wholesome picture on meditation it is critical that we educate ourselves a bit about the underlying ancient philosophy upon which it is built. This knowledge is profoundly deep and powerful, and understanding which will totally change the way you think about meditation. Your confusion will turn into clarity and your skepticism will turn into a solid belief and excitement. The next two sections of the chapter will shed some light on this subject. Keeping it short and crisp I outline the basic idea.

3.2 - Ancient Wisdom on Workings of The Mind

"You cannot take control of your life as long as you remain prisoner in your conditioned mind."

In the preceding chapter I covered the importance of taking the inner journey and highlighted the importance of 'lowering the number of thoughts' as a precondition to being able to quiet the mind and thus being able to realize the many benefits of meditation practice. The monkey-mind is running around in perpetual motion from one thought to another. Requesting the mind to stop, or commanding the thoughts to stop won't make them stop. "Thinking your way out of thoughts is like trying to get out of quicksand by pulling yourself up by a hair. At the bottom of any thought, however positive, is still a canyon of more thoughts."[2] That is why trying to change or rearrange your thoughts won't help you calm your emotional struggle. The only way this mindless running around of the senses and the train of thoughts could be stopped, is by withdrawing the charge, and cutting off the fuel supply that feeds the thinking machine.

In order to understand *how* you stop the incessant mind chatter, and perhaps the only way to understand this, we must take a look at India's ancient scriptures that explain the workings of the mind. Only by understanding the 'inner' workings of the human mind would it be possible to fix an 'outwardly' problem. I touch upon this otherwise lofty subject to give you a brief idea about the foundational principles of meditation-practice, and I do so by summarizing the content into three short sections of Samkhya philosophy, Levels of the Mind, and Prana-Yoga concept.

3.2.1. Samkhya Philosophy, Summarized

The content here is authentic as it is researched and compiled out of the works of multiple expert sources*. Learning about the inner workings of the mind founded on 'Samkhya Philosophy' will provide a perspective that would help you appreciate the inherent scientific and psychological basis for practicing meditation. Without getting into too deep I will give you only the leading ideas on this philosophy. You might find the content here as it pertains to ancient philosophy a bit difficult to absorb without deep reflection. But don't be alarmed, for the logical sequence with which I summarize, and simplify really, the concept in a step-by-step manner will make it easy for you to grasp the concept without being overwhelmed. I suggest you keep an open mind and browse through each point slowly, taking a pause to reflect on what you read before moving to the next point.

You will see the basis of what the modern scientists are objectively measuring in the labs using scanners and sensors today was subjectively discovered by the ancient yogis who documented their experiences (darshanas) in the ancient texts. "The Samkhya was based on reason and proof. And the foundation of this philosophy was secular, based on empirical studies, not opinions."[65]

1. According to the Samkhya system, the way we perceive the world, the way we participate in this world, all of our experiences and our existence, is governed by two 'Eternal Principles' of:
    a. *Purusha* (poo-roo-shaa), and
    b. *Prakriti* (pra-kree-tee).

2. The Purusha is: Unchanging; Undisturbed; Unconditioned; Unmanifested; Formless; Self; The Spirit; **The Higher Mind**. The Prakriti is: Changing; Disturbed; Conditioned; Manifested; The Creative Power; The field of forces of the mind; The mind-matter-energy; **The Lower Mind**.

   Together, the *Purusha* and the *Prakriti* represent our core identity in the whole universe and is termed as *Brahman* (Bra-Ha-Mann).

3. *Purusha* are many, yet identical. *Prakriti* is one, a continuum. The *Purusha* is a universal **Psychical principle**. It is the omnipresent, everlasting, and the realm of the immortal. *Prakriti* is a universal **Physical principle**, the realm of birth and death.
4. Both *Purusha* and *Prakriti* have three qualities each, also known as their attributes or characteristics. The *Purusha* has-
   a. Awareness,
   b. Life-Force (Prana, Chi) and,
   c. Immutability or Eternity.

   * Ref. numbers 9,10,30,31,33,41

   The *Prakriti* has

   a. Rhythm (Sattva),
   b. Mobility (Rajas), and
   c. Inertia (Tamas).

The three attributes of *Prakriti* - Sattva, Rajas, and Tamas- are Sanskrit words in the original scriptures representing an extremely popular aspect of everyday life in Indian cultures, that of "*gunas*" (goo-naa-s). The *gunas* are the evolutionary powers that also define the psychic and the physical nature of a person. In short, Sattva represents purity and balance, Rajas represents activity, and Tamas represents ignorance.

5. The *Prakriti*, which I earlier noted to be the 'field of forces of the mind', is broken down into 24 Tattvas (or principles) which represent our world and the overall experience of our life.

   5 Elements- Earth, Water, Fire, Air, Space
   5 Sense Objects- Eyes, Ears, Nose, Tongue, Skin
   5 Senses- Seeing, Hearing, Smell, Taste, Touch (sensory powers of the internal world)
   5 Action Organs- Hands, Legs, Larynx, Excretion, Reproduction
   3 Mental Phenomena- Memory, Intellect and Ego (Power of Conception), and
   1 Universal Energy: The Life Force

6. The *Purusha* is unable to do anything by itself. It animates and vitalizes *Prakriti* and stirs its evolutionary powers into motion. When Purusha comes near *Prakriti* then under *Purusha's* influence the *Prakriti* begins to live, begins to change, and brings about the manifestation of multitude of forms in the universe.

   When Awareness in *Purusha* is reflected in Rhythm (Sattva) of *Prakriti*, the influence is 'Cognition'.

   When Prana in Purusha is reflected in Mobility (Rajas) in Prakriti, the influence is 'Activity.'

   When Eternity in Purusha is reflected in Inertia (Tamas) in Prakriti, the influence becomes 'Will or Desire.'

7. COGNITION, ACTIVITY, and WILL is the holy trinity of our existence and the grounds of our consciousness. That is all there is.
   COGNITION is the power to know; I know,
   ACTIVITY is the power to manifest; I act;
   WILL is the power to resolve; I desire.

8. In everything that exists in the universe, in both the outer world and the inner world (a concept covered in chapter 1) there is an interplay of the three powers of cognition, activity and will. In that mix, one power has a predominance over others, and which results in a multitude of manifestations and diversity of forms.

   Pure COGNITION mixed with ACTIVITY and WILL, gives rise to the mental body: the thinking principle.

   Think of it as the inner chambers of the mind. And importantly, meditation is mainly concerned with this mental body as described in the figure below.

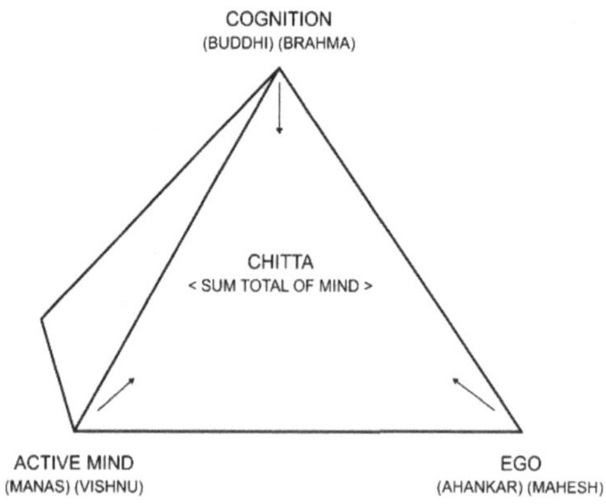

[In his book Inner Engineering, Sadhguru explains, "CHITTA is the basis of our lives. It is the deepest level of the mind. It is the awareness, aliveness, a profound intelligence that lies beyond memory, beyond intellect, beyond judgment, beyond all divisions, and beyond all identities. It is the intelligence of existence itself, the living mind of cosmos."]

9. The main definition of meditation in Sanskrit is "Chitta Vrutti Nirodha", meaning the dissolution/cessation/neutralization of patterns of disturbances/mental phenomena that incessantly rise and fall in human consciousness. And it is a journey from manifestation (small Self, lower mind) to the Brahman (pure Self, higher mind).

   Yoga guru B.K.S Iyengar says, "The life of an ordinary man is filled with an unending series of disturbances and frustrations and with the reactions to them. It is by coordinated efforts of my body and mind that I obtain the prize of inner peace and fulfil the quest of the soul to meet the maker."

This is in brief the idea behind the Samkhya philosophy. You may do your own research and find out more as to how it relates to mediation practice. For now, as a beginner in meditation, keep in mind the image of "Chitta", the mind principle which is the central focus area of our mediation practice.

3.2.2 The Levels of the Mind

"The traveller has to knock at every alien door to come to his own and one has to wander through all the outer worlds to reach the innermost shrine at the end." -- from the poem "Journey Home" by Rabindranath Tagore

"You have fallen into the machinery of your own mind."[40]

The ancient sages applied Samkhya principles in their own practice and discovered that the mind has multiple layers from which arises the mental disturbances of different kind. With experimentation and self-examination they realized that as you go deeper, layer by layer, there comes a point where all the mental phenomena gradually comes to a stop. And at this point you experience the grand silence, that of a deep ocean. This insight made them realize that in order to slow down or stop the thinking process, you must dive through each layer beneath the level from which all the mental disturbances spring. They also realized that by bringing awareness within us and making the mind as still as an untouched mountain lake, one can experience an unending peace, joy, happiness, and wisdom.

Imagine your mind, the mental body, in the shape of an ICEBERG as shown in the figure below - ICEBERG LEVELS:

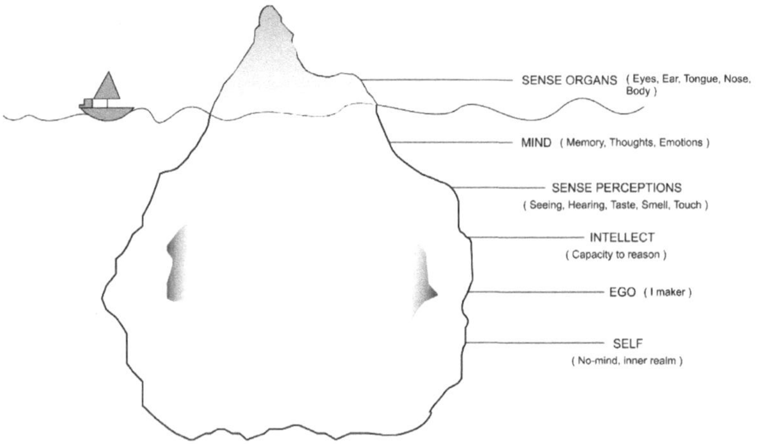

These levels of the iceberg represent the different modes of our mental existence, also known as mental formations in Buddhist terminology. Our normal day waking-state consciousness is at the surface, at the level of senses and sense perceptions. At this level there is a constant flux and constant motion where the waves of thoughts, desires and emotions are constantly rising and falling in our minds.

As you go deeper, more and more interesting levels start to show up. Below the surface, the realm of thoughts, emotions, memories, intellect, conditioning, and the Ego make up these deeper layers of the mind. And beyond these levels, near the bottom of the iceberg lies the realm of no-mind. Our experiences of daily life in the waking state are only a fragment of possibilities that exist at deeper levels.

In order to reach the deepest level, every level of the active mind above it must be transcended, one by one. You approach one level, rest it, and move deeper to the next. And you repeat the process until you address the entire iceberg. When all the mental phenomena come to an end, there emerges the flow state. This is the state of an unburdened mind. This is where you discover your true nature of infinite wisdom, power, love, compassion, joy, intuition, creativity, peace and above all, that of grand awareness.

In order to dive through each layer, the mind needs a vehicle, and the vehicle is MEDITATION. In meditation you stop every mode in which the mind manifests itself. You disidentify with mental formations, layer-by-layer: I am not my thoughts, I am not my emotions, I am not my intellect, I am not my ego, I am not my body. And that is how you arrive at SELF, your true nature. The functions of the mind must be suppressed, and the states of mind must be inhibited in order to experience the quietude of the mind and tranquillity of the senses. Meditation is the method of producing this quietude by directing consciousness beneath the level from which all the mental disturbances arise. Sheath after sheath has to be transcended, like peeling through the layers of an onion, to the point where nothing can stir your mind, nothing can bother you. Author Deepak Chopra says, "Instead of subduing a drunken monkey the appropriate metaphor for meditation is much more like creeping through a herd of sleeping elephants without waking them up."

Deepening consciousness is not something that is reserved for sages and saints of the east. This possibility is available to all of us simply by practicing breathing meditation (Pranayama). With a daily and disciplined meditation practice, simply doing breathing meditation exercises and yoga, anyone can deepen their consciousness, reach the bottom of the iceberg, and experience supreme peace and connectedness.

3.2.3 Prana And Yoga Concept

"Abundant Prana means greater resilience, greater resources of energy for weathering the storms and stresses of life."[10]

Before we look into the various definitions of meditation and clearly articulate what meditation-practice is all about, let us take a quick detour to review the concepts of "Prana" and "Yoga". For a beginner especially, the knowledge of these two foundational principles will provide a new perspective on meditation that is both encouraging and exciting.

The Sanskrit word "Prana" means the life-force, and is essentially an ancient theory of energy. Any discussion on meditation and Yoga in any form will invariably include the word "Prana" (pronounced Praa+Na), and the same concept exists in different cultures, as Chinese Chi, Japanese Ki, Greek Pneuma, Hebrews Ruah, and so on. As per yoga philosophy the breath (breathing) does not just bring in air filled with oxygen, hydrogen and nitrogen, but it brings in life-force, the Prana, a subtle dynamic substance that causes growth, vitality, motion, repairs the body, heals injuries, and cures diseases.[33] It is this energy that creates and sustains everything in the universe from planets and celestial bodies to the insides of an atom. Charles Darwin called it the sensorial energy, and the other various connotations for Prana includes: 'the vital-force, the active principle of life, active principle of vitality, the universal principle of force, the universal principle of energy, the absolute energy.'

Just as the oxygenated blood is carried to all parts of the body, building up and replenishing, so is the Prana carried to all parts of the nervous system, adding strength and vitality[30]. However, since there is no chemical trace for Prana it doesn't register on any scientific instruments, making it a hard-to-digest concept for a Western mind. With every breath the Prana moves around like wind, and with the energy of the Sun drawn from the right nostril and the energy of the Moon drawn from the left nostril, it is distributed all over the body through the central channel and system of Chakras (see 3.4.3).

The ancient Yoga system proposes that through proper use and control of Prana one can reach higher states of consciousness, and attain many powers associated with an unburdened mind.[57] This act and ability to control Prana as a matter of regulating the inhalation and exhalation and the pauses between breaths is defined as "Pranayama" (also a technical term for "breathing meditation"). This Sanskrit term was coined by ancient yogic sage Patanjali who is considered to be the father of yoga and meditation, and it is made of two words Prana + Ayama. The word Prana means life-force or breath, and Ayama means control, stretching, discipline or science.

The ancient yogis spent thousands of years honing the Pranayama techniques. They were able to store the Prana in the Solar plexus (aka abdominal brain) just as a battery stores electricity, and many powers are attributed to intelligent use of this stored up energy. In Hawaii there are native kahuna doctors that use the life energy concept of 'mana' in their healing practices. The 'Ha' is the sacred breath of life within all of us and breathing practice is called 'ha huna'. By breathing deeply and visualizing mana, there is a positive effect on wellbeing, physical strength, senses and the mind.[39]

The **Pranayama** is one of the eight limbs of the "Astanga Yoga path (eight-limbed path)" of a comprehensive yoga system called the "Yoga Sutras of Patanjali". These sutras, or threads, outline a system for us to follow for our spiritual evolution and living a happier and healthier life. It is the primary text for all the various types of meditation and yoga practices that flourish today in their myriads of forms.[47] These sutras (threads) range from 5000 BC to 300 AD. The word Yoga literally means "union" and the science of yoga is to be in perfect harmony with existence. Human development as per this system is multifaceted and dependent on not just one, but multiple factors together, such as moral development, character building, ethical behavior, physical health, mental health and spiritual development. At its core, the Astanga yoga path supports an aspirant in drawing consciousness from external focus to an inward focus. Many other wisdom traditions and religious scriptures, both of the East and the West prescribe some or the other form of moral code of conduct. However, nothing comes close to the holistic and wholesome perspective as the one prescribed in the yoga sutras.

The eight limbs of Yoga are as follows:

1. Yama: The ethical discipline, the universal moral commandments; Non-hurting; No stealing; Truthfulness; Self -control; Non-possessiveness; Letting go.
2. Niyama: The rules to apply in daily life; self-purification by discipline; cleanliness; hygiene; contentment; gratitude; discipline; responsible behaviour; Faith and devotion.
3. Asana: The physical yoga posture practice, one which is more popular around the world; The physical postures serve as a physical exercise and mental discipline.
4. Pranayama: Regulation of breath; Yogic breathing (detailed in 3.4.4).
5. Pratyahara: Sense withdrawal; persistent effort and repetition of effort in order to dis-identify the mind from the body, senses, thinking and ego; to abstract oneself from distractions.
6. Dhaarana: Concentration; reached when effort to dis-identify mind from the confines of mental phenomena is finally successful and is about to become steadfast and one-pointed.
7. Dhyana: The meditative state; Deepened consciousness.
8. Samadhi: Transcendence from mind to no-mind; Enlightened state.

Meditation is essentially concerned with limbs #4 through #8. In order to explain these elements in a way that would make it easy for a new seeker to understand, I use the following analogy from the sport of surfing.

PRANAYAMA - Getting in the ocean
PRATYAHARA - Paddling out
DHARANA - Catching the wave
DHYANA - Riding the wave
SAMADHI - Becoming the wave

3.3 - Meditation Is All About This

"All weather comes and goes
And no storm ever hurt the sky.
That's the meditative mind."

We came full circle, starting with "Is this book for you?" setting expectations about the powers of meditation-practice, then moving on to understand the WHY of meditation with the urgency of "Run Forrest Run", and after navigating the problems of the outer and inner worlds, we arrived at the doorstep of meditation, identifying it as a powerful and transformative tool to be used in order to solve the inner-world conflicts. We further explored the many benefits of meditation-practice and parsed through the scientific research outcomes confirming these benefits. We also covered the ancient philosophy and science behind meditation, along with understanding the workings of the mind and the levels of consciousness by using the example of an iceberg.

The journey so far, along with the unique perspective presented by weaving the ancient wisdom, science, philosophy, and my personal story on meditation, has given you, as I would like to believe, a fairly good idea about what meditation and its practice is all about.

There is no one standardized way of defining meditation. Different people define it in different ways based on their personal beliefs and experience, in their own unique language and ways of expression. Some may call it a method to relax your mind, some say it's a process to deepen your consciousness, some term it as a spiritual pursuit to achieve enlightenment, some word it as an exploration of the inner realm, and so on. These various definitions and the pathways for the expression of a concept, at the end, converge onto one core definition and purpose of meditation, which is originally worded by Sri Patanjali as "Chitta Vrutti Nirodha", (pronounced Cheet+ta, Vru+tee, Neer+o+dha).

It means that there are various states of mind (Chitta) where the mental disturbances of various kinds (thoughts, sensations, emotions, feelings, memories, reasoning, intellect, judgments, ego) rise and fall in our consciousness. And this is the tendency (Vrutti) of a conditioned mind. However, there are also states of mind where thinking stops and mental disturbances cease (Nirodha). And that there are ways to stop thinking and come to a silent state of mind (Meditation). Simply put, quieting and balancing the mental conflicts of a conditioned mind. In the various definitions of meditation and meditation-practice presented in this segment you will see a common thread running through each and gravitating towards the core definition.

Meditation is the training of the mind to develop mental qualities and develop strength for solving the mind's self-inflicted problems of stress, anxiety, fear, suffering and negative thinking.[20] In addition to breathing, the traditional practices also incorporate the elements of repetition, relaxation, Mantra chanting, finger movements, intention, and faith. The primary goal of meditation is to transition from a burdened mind to an unburdened mind. Just as the Sun is periodically obscured by the drifting dark clouds, the same way our true Self is obscured by mind's conditioning, and meditation is the method for removing these mental clouds and discovering our true nature.

"In meditation we reach the state of dreamless sleep where the nervous system rests and the body repairs itself, and the mind is refreshed. We enter this state wakefully and this process of healing and rejuvenation goes at a deeper level in both body and mind."[10] Author Deepak Chopra calls meditation the art of doing nothing, and notes, "When I sit in meditation, my inner experience can be described by what I am not doing. I am not focusing, I am not monitoring, I am not thinking, I am not reacting, I am not in action. I am getting the activity of the mind to turn into silence without forcing it to do so."[2]

Meditation is the 'unfolding process' by which you deepen your attention and awareness. You come to meditation to listen carefully to the silence between your thoughts, to your heart, to your breathing, to just be present without having to go anywhere or make anything better. As the awareness deepens in meditation you can see clearly where the stress is coming from, where the anger, resentment, bitterness, guilt, frustration, and all the suffering is coming from, and then let go of it, release it effectively and achieve restfulness.

From its origins in Indian philosophical and psychological systems of ancient times and in its most traditional sense, the meditation is USE OF BREATH AS AN EXERCISE, as a vehicle, to travel not only around the surface but across the entire mind-vertical [refer Section 3.2.2]. And 'by changing your breath you change what goes on in your mind', is the central premise for meditation-practice. By becoming aware of our breath and using our breath we cultivate the qualities of restfulness, calmness, peace, concentration, focus, joy, and happiness. "Because of the mind's tendency to be scattered and be easily distracted by daydreams and thoughts, we use breath to help anchor to the present. By repeatedly coming back to rest in breath we are countering the forces of distraction."[20] This trains the mind, heart and body to become settled and unified on one thing, at one place, at one time.

"It is your mind that determines the quality of your life, and it is your energy that determines the state of your mind, and it is your breath (Prana) that determines the quality of your energy."[5] Therefore, this connection of BREATH (Prana) --> ENERGY --> STATE OF MIND --> QUALITY OF LIFE is the key to mastering your mind. Breathing is the fastest and simplest way to invite more Prana into your system and naturally shift into calmness.

The bottom line is that any meditation practice is about one just one thing— quieting the mind. It is about stillness of your mind. It is only in stillness and inner silence that you are drawn to something greater than you and you can cross over into something majestic and limitless. Only in stillness one can experience lasting peace and love and joy. Only in the moments of thought-free awareness can one experience clarity, intuition and wisdom flowing through you. This parable from the book "Spiritual Anatomy by Daaji" sums up this definition so beautifully—

"One day Buddha asked his disciples to bring him a cup of water from a nearby pond. When they returned with water, Buddha asked them to drink it. However, the water was dirty and murky so they could not drink it. Buddha told them to set the cup aside and wait. After some time the dirt settled to the bottom, and the water above became clear and drinkable." Stillness creates clarity. And it creates space for self-purification.

3.4 - Core Elements of Meditation Practice

In the earlier segment while clearing the misconceptions about meditation we saw that there are several broad categories of meditation practice, such as Focused Attention, Awareness Training, TM, Vipassana, Mindfulness Meditation, and many others. Each of these forms and its sub-forms contain a unique structure of its own, with its unique methods that include a set of exercises you perform as part of the practice. At the end, each form is designed to lead the meditator into the quietude of the inner realm. Now while there are significant differences between each, there are also some similarities and common elements across these practices, which I call the "Core Elements" of meditation practice. Every form and type of meditation practice that exists in the market will include some or all of the six core elements. It might exist as an "input" to the process or as an "outcome" of the process. For example, in candle meditation your input is "focus and concentration" and the outcome is "relaxation". I elaborate upon the six core elements in this segment.

The type of meditation I preach and practice contains all six of these core elements, and I include them in my "SoZo Meditation" program as well. This is everything a beginner really needs to know, and I believe it is also the best way to begin your meditation journey.

The six core elements are:

1. Intention and Faith
2. Concentration and Awareness
3. Sitting Posture (Attitude)
4. Breath Mastery (Focus)
5. Chanting Mantra (Repetition)
6. Relaxation

This is not a perfect analogy, but in the physical fitness world I would compare it to a full-body workout. Some workouts are targeted to one specific body area or muscle group, such as upper body, lower body, biceps, triceps, back, shoulders, core, legs, cardio, and so on. While there are some workouts that engage and target multiple muscle groups at a time, such as burpees, push-ups, and so on. My "SoZo Meditation" program is based on the full-body workout concept, and includes all the six core elements of traditional practices. As the meaning of these core elements becomes clear to you, the way you think about meditation practice will change from skepticism to excitement.

3.4.1 Intention & Faith

A fairly common definition of intention is- a strong purpose or aim, accompanied by a strong determination to produce a desired result. In order to achieve anything meaningful in life you have to have a clear purpose, a burning desire, and a hefty amount of faith in your mission and in God of your belief. It starts with the right intent and right attitude.

The first step in your meditation practice should be that of setting intention. This is no fixed way or standard requirement defined by Buddha or Patanjali for starting your meditation practice. But you should not straightway jump into breathing exercises and chanting mantras, say, without getting your mind and body ready for the practice. Just as doing some stretches and warm up exercises before beginning a physical workout greatly increases the efficiency of your workout, the same way a mental warm up of sorts will ensure a productive meditation practice. And the easiest and most efficient way to get your mind and body ready for meditation, to get in the zone, is by setting your intention.

It is like an airplane positioning itself on the runway at the right spot, at the right angle, at the right speed, in the right gear, ready for take-off. You declare your intention to the universe, and seek strength from the universe to support you in your undertaking. Just as the sitting posture gets your body in position for meditation, setting intention gets your mind in the right position for meditation. It is an expression of your sincere desire and a strong commitment to practice meditation every day. It is a ritual you follow every time you sit in practice. The ritual may include taking a deep long breath, asking the universe for guidance, to give you strength, to bless you, so that you are able to perform meditation with a deep commitment and joy, so that everything goes well, so that the practice is fruitful, and you reap the benefits of meditating.

In Indian culture there is an age-old custom of setting your intention and it is known as "Sankalpa". The Sanskrit word "Sankalpa", pronounced as sun+cull+pa, has multiple meanings like setting intention, promise, decision-making, determination, desire, prayer, or positivity. The act of setting Sankalpa is performed before commencing every important undertaking in life, small or big, an important mission, a project, or any goal-oriented task such as, an exam, sports event, marriage, adventure, workout session, meditation session, stage performance, travel, surgery, and so on. It is an act of establishing an attitude of doing all you need to do in pursuit of your goal, of moving forward in spite of the challenges, and of anchoring your faith in the God of your belief. In my “SoZo Meditation” program the first exercise you will perform in the first one minute of your practice is always that of setting intention. A clear guidance, including an example and step-by-step instructions on how to perform this exercise is covered in chapter 6.

3.4.2. Concentration And Awareness

The human attention span is getting shorter and shorter, and it is becoming harder and harder for most to concentrate on a particular activity for more than a few seconds at stretch. I hear this every day from so many people, "Bro, I cannot focus for a minute on anything...", "It's impossible to concentrate on one thing for long, the mind keeps running here and there", "I cannot sit still in one place for over a minute", and so on. One of the main benefits of meditation is that it helps us build back our focus and concentration, and which in turn helps us perform our daily tasks with greater awareness and patience.

Many of the mindfulness meditation practices and some other forms of meditation require that you focus your attention intensely upon a particular object. You become aware of the various aspects of that object, and slowly and gradually merge into the object to become one with it. For example, in a candle meditation form, you focus your attention on a burning candle. You observe and become aware of the flame, the movement of the flames, the colour of the flames, and you hold your attention firmly on the candle for minutes and hours. The advanced practitioners are able to reach a state where the subject (meditator) completely merges into the object (candle and flame) and experience the feeling of immense joy and peace. Some beginners may also experience fleeting glimpses of such a state, but the ability to hold your focus and awareness comes only through intense practice. The Buddhas and the enlightened beings are able to routinely enter such a state at will, even when they are not meditating.

If the object of your focus is an image of a God of your belief, an idol, a photo, you can become aware and observe the object's qualities as reflected in that particular image. If the object of your focus is your thoughts, you become aware of the origins of your thoughts and observe the thought without reacting. You treat your thoughts like visitors entering your room from one door and exiting from the other. You may label it, name it, but you don't react and let it pass through without friction of any kind.

The problem with such focused-attention and monitoring forms of meditation is that they require a lot of mental effort, and it is quite counterintuitive to ask an already distracted, agitated, restless, unsettled and unfocused mind to intensely focus upon a certain object. The fact is that many such practices were originally designed for monks and monastery life, and which is only one of the many activities and programs practiced by monks over the course of their typical day. These activities work collectively as a whole, in an integrated way. For people like us, not living in monasteries, but in a fast-paced modern world with busy and stress-ridden lives, these practices, when performed in isolation, may not produce the desired results. More so because we do not possess the necessary mindset, discipline, patience and the right environment as that of a monk. Many of these Eastern practices packaged for Western consumption by the various commercial entities are therefore rarely successful with the new seekers.

The more you try to concentrate and focus, as an "input" in your practice, the more energy drain you will experience. The more you chase concentration, the more it eludes you. You have to let it happen. You have to let it come to you, as an "output" of the process. And this is what I discovered in my own practice. In my opinion, concentration and awareness are mainly, and should be, an outcome of your meditation practice, and not an input. More than it being an input in the process, something that you need beforehand to be able to perform meditation practice, it is instead an ensued benefit of the practice.

There are various different exercises included in my “SoZo Meditation” program for you, and none of them requires or demands intense focusing, monitoring or labelling. Furthermore, if someone tries to convince you that a particular form of meditation is effortless, then you must first understand what that really means. As you dive deeper in meditation with whatever form and type you choose to practice, and when you reach a state where your mind is calm and the thoughts have slowed down, you feel connected, and everything happening to you in that state, everything you do in that state, just feels effortless. You are in a state of an expanded concentration and awareness.

Cultivating focus and concentration has significant benefits for daily life such as, increased productivity, improved academic performance, better quality of work, immersing fully into something, greater intuition, creativity, improved attention span, success at jobs and career, and so on.

3.4.3 Sitting Posture (Attitude)

How you use your body in meditation, the way you sit, your body positioning, your posture, is an important consideration in performing meditation-practice. A posture embodies wakefulness. To take a posture itself is the right state of mind and your body affirms, radiates and broadcasts an attitude of presence and readiness. The posture represents an intention, a commitment, and an acceptance of whatever comes in the moment. The Yogic breathing exercises and chanting Mantras are generally performed in a sitting position and there is a specific way you sit in meditation. Sitting reinforces being awake and conscious. If for some reason, medical or otherwise, sitting is a difficult ask, then some of the exercises can be performed in a lying-down or standing position.

The simple rule for sitting in meditation is - your head, neck and spine must be aligned in a straight line. Simply put, sit as straight as you can. In doing so you must be comfortable and not feel any strain or tension in your body. As for the 'sitting' part, you may choose to sit on the floor on a meditation mat, a yoga mat, a carpet, or on a chair, a bench or a stool. The 5 most common ways to sit in meditation are as follows -

(1) Full lotus, (2) Half lotus, (3) Seiza (Japanese style), (4) Tailor or cross-legged, and (5) Sitting on chair

In addition to the positioning of your legs, the placement of your hands is also important. In yogic tradition the hand-palm-finger placement is called a "mudra". And there are 4 common mudras that can be applied into your practice as follows –

(1) Thumb and First, (2) Palms resting over Thigh, (3) Palm resting over Palm, and (4) Namaste.

A picture is worth a thousand words and the following images will give you a clear idea about these various postures.

Half lotus front view with gyan mudra

Half lotus front view with palms on palms buddhist mudra

Simple cross-legged front view with namaste mudra

Seiza front view with palms on lap facing up

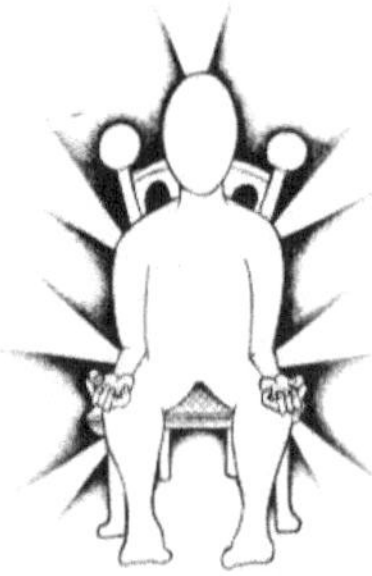

Sitting on a chair in front view with gyan mudra.

A Word on Chakras:

Without getting into any details, I cover a minimalist introduction of the "Chakras" concept as it relates to sitting meditation and yogic breathing. If you are interested in getting a more in-depth knowledge on the subject then I'd encourage you to do your own research.

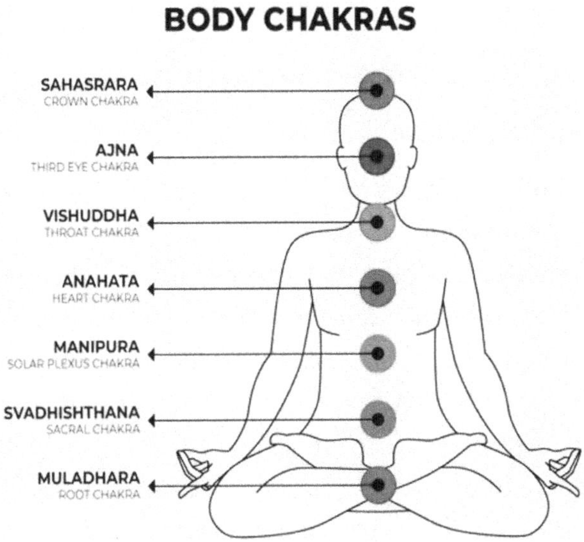

The "Chakras" (plural for Chakra), pronounced as chuck+raas, is a Sanskrit word that means "Spinning Wheels". They are the energy centers that are vertically aligned along the central axis of the body from base of the spine to the crown of the head.[53] According to Hindu metaphysical systems Chakras are the traditional energy centers of the Astral body. They represent another nonphysical, subtle, energy-type body that interpenetrates the physical body.[52] Out of a total 114 Chakras, there are 12 main Chakras, and 7 of which are designated as root Chakras. These seven root Chakras roughly correspond to a specific location in the physical body as shown in the figure above.

#1 Lies at the point between anus and genitals

#2 Lies at the root of genitals

#3 Corresponds to Solar plexus

#4 Near the heart

#5 Throat region

#6 Slightly behind the space between eyebrows

#7 Above the crown of the head

The symbolism of Chakras represents an internal road map, a spiritual maturation process that can lead us from the unconscious to the conscious mind, then to the superconscious.[53] The vital-force (Prana) is channeled through the subtle body via tubes which are similar to veins and arteries, called Nadis in Sanskrit, and distributed across the body. The Chinese medical practice of acupuncture is founded on the same language of energy. One of the main reasons for sitting straight in meditation is so that the Chakras are aligned and that way Prana can irrigate all the channels with maximum efficiency.

The seven Chakras are commonly pictured as lotus blossoms with petals, or as spinning wheels with spokes, and each petal or spoke vibrates at a unique frequency of its own. And it is believed that the Chakras when purified and opened up through the practice of yoga and meditation leads the practitioner to experience mental, physical and spiritual transformation. In a healthy person, the Chakras are vibrant and spin with vigour. In an unhealthy person they are sluggish and only partially opened. These outcomes were carefully written down in the Vedas, the Upanishads, and most recently the Sutras of Patanjali.[52]

Lastly, you must know that the sounds chanted in mantra in certain sequences result in a vibrational effect upon the chakras and the physical body. As the practitioner works with mantra over days, months, and even years there is a steady accumulation of energy and the Prana grows more vibrant and powerful.

3.4.4 Breath Mastery (Focus)

The first thing you do when you come to life is breathe-in, and the last thing you do before you die is breathe-out. The Bible describes in Genesis 2:1 how the Lord God created man from the dust of the ground, and breathed into his nostril the breath of life, and the man became a living soul. We can survive without food and water for days, but only a few moments without breath. Clearly, your breath is the doorway to both life and death, and therefore breathing has to be a lot more than just a passive function of lungs.

Breathing is so much more than just getting air in our bodies. In a single breath tens of billions of air molecules pass through our nose, affecting nearly every internal organ in the body and the bodily functions. The inhale and exhale happens over 50,000 times each day where about 3000 gallons (11,000 litres) of air travels through 14900 miles (23,000 km) of airways in the body. Millions of life-sustaining complex biochemical processes are taking place inside our body with every breath cycle, and without us feeling any effort.

The breath is clearly our simplest, yet most intimate connection to our environment. And as noted in the section about Prana in the previous chapter, the breath invites not just oxygen, nitrogen and hydrogen, but also Prana, the vital force which fuels our existence and sustenance of the entire universe. And Pranayama (breath meditation) is the process of controlling the flow of the Prana. Research shows that an average person at rest takes about 16 breaths per minute, 960 per hour, 23,040 per day, 8,409,600 per year, and more than 100 million over a lifetime.[57] Just imagine the wonderful powers an intelligent use and control of your breathing can bring to you.

Furthermore, have you ever noticed how your emotions, attitudes, and concerns are expressed in the way you breathe? The way we breathe affects our bodies in different ways. Subtle changes in breath are often a sign of subtle changes in the mind. When you are angry and restless your breath is constricted, shallow, fast, forced, and hot. When you are feeling calm or when you are deep in concentration your breath is slow, steady and deep. Just as your feelings affect your breathing, the same way your breathing can affect how you feel. It's a two-way street. The age-old advice "just breathe", or "take a deep breath" when stressed or angry means that deep breathing can instantly calm an agitated and tense mind.

In the fast-paced and uber-connected world, however, we have forgotten to breathe, and breathe the right way. Universal awareness of the importance of breathing does not exist and in modern times we seem to have lost touch with our breath. In his must-read book Breath, author James Nestor notes, "Scientists have discovered that our capacity to breathe has changed through the long process of human evolution, and the way we breathe has gotten markedly worse since the dawn of the industrial age." We have contracted improper methods of breathing and because of which we have withered chests, stooping shoulders and arched backs, and a terrible rise of respiratory diseases. The physicians report that humans use less than 30 percent of their lung capacity, and not utilizing the entire breathing apparatus leads to ill health and respiratory issues. Which means we are not breathing optimally.

Optimal breathing is full, free, and uninhibited breathing using the full range of our breathing apparatus. "A typical adult engages only 10% or less of the range of diaphragm when breathing - which overburdens the heart, elevates blood pressure, and causes a rash of respiratory problems."[65] The quality of your breath, the way you breathe, profoundly affects your quality of life, the quality of inner energy, and your nervous system. If you want to find out more about the breath and breathing- evolutionary history, science, philosophy, biochemistry, physiology, and more, I recommend reading this extraordinary book "Breath - The New A Science Of A Lost Art" by James Nestor. The way you think about breath and meditation will change for ever.

Use of breath as an exercise, and as a way to calm your mind and improve your concentration is what breathing meditation is all about. Breath meditation is about becoming aware of your breathing and bringing consciousness to your breathing. Breath creates presence. All Eastern cultures for centuries have used Breathing as a healing tool, in various breathing-meditation forms, therapeutic practices, and spiritual pursuits. "Seven books of Chinese Tao dating back around 400 BCE focused entirely on breathing and how to use your breath."[65] Breath is the simplest and most efficient tool we have to control our minds. By repeatedly and rhythmically coming back to rest in breath we are countering the strong forces of distraction and mental disturbances.[19] An intelligent control and use of your breathing will train your mind-heart-body to become settled and unified in one thing, and help cultivate steadiness of mind.

There is a wide variety of ways you can breathe in meditation. The different styles and patterns of breathing become your breathing exercises, popularly termed as 'rhythmic breathing' or 'yoga breathing'. These various patterns of breathing are -- Breathing slow and deep, emphasizing inhalation and exhalation; Breathing fast and shallow; Breathing smooth, rough or constricted; Intentionally pausing between the breaths; Holding breath after inhalation and exhalation; Changing intensity and speed of breathing; Inhale via one nostril and exhale via other; Breathing from the back of your throat feeling the air touching the roof of your palate; and so on.

The various different ways of breathing affect your mind-body in different ways and have a definite science associated with them as noted below (from online resource).

- Slow breathing triggers the body's relaxation response. It also increases dopamine levels in different parts of the brain in just the first ten minutes of meditation.
- Deep breathing decreases the activity in the frontal lobes, lowers CO_2 levels in the blood, and reduces cognitive activity and blood flow from different parts of the brain. Simply put, it calms your mind.
- Slow and deep breathing calms amygdala (a part of the emotional brain), counteracts past-future response, relaxes muscles, warms hands, and regulates the heart's rhythms.
- Rapid breathing has a stimulating effect on the limbic system of the brain and can trigger a variety of emotional release.

Learn Yogic Breathing

Breathing in meditation is termed as yogic-breathing or meditator's breathing. It is also known as diaphragmatic breathing. It is not hard to learn how to breathe in meditation.

We convert the automatic activity of daily breathing that happens without our conscious effort and awareness into a conscious activity of rhythmic breathing. Before I describe the proper way to breathe in meditation let us quickly review the physiology of breathing which we learnt in our science class in elementary school.

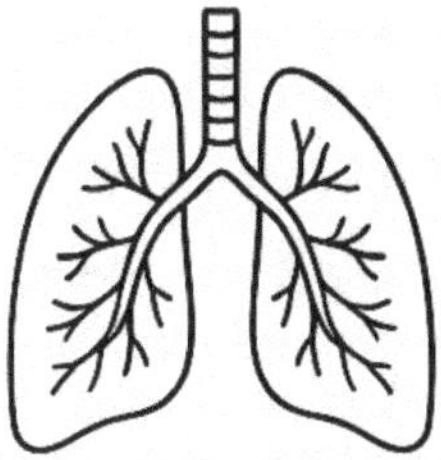

The air passage consists of the interior of nasal passage, pharynx, larynx, windpipe or trachea and the bronchial tubes. The air is drawn into lungs by the action of the diaphragm, a flat sheet-like muscle, stretched across the chest, sitting between the chest-bone and abdomen. The diaphragm's action is almost as automatic as that of the heart. "When the diaphragm expands, it increases the size of the chest and lungs as the air rushes into the vacuum that is created. When the diaphragm relaxes, the chest and lungs contract and air is expelled from the lungs."[33] The breath delivers Oxygen from the atmosphere into the lungs where it is picked up by your bloodstream and taken to all the cells in your whole body. And breathing allows elimination of waste products such as CO_2.

Anyone wanting to learn more about yogic-breathing should read the book The Hindu Yogic Science Of Breath, by Yogi Ramacharaka, where the mechanics of yogic-breathing is explained in greater detail. "The yogic-breathing brings the whole breathing apparatus into play: every part of the lungs, chest, diaphragm, and all muscles in the respiratory process from abdomen through groin is used fully. The Yogic breath consists of three distinct movements which, although technically separate, merge into one uniform movement without any force or breaks or abrupt movements. These three movements relate to the lower, middle and upper portions of the lungs."[33] Let's give it a quick try. It's easy.

Step 1: Breathe via nostrils; first filling up the *lower* part of lungs, which is accompanied by bringing into play the diaphragm, which descends to push forward the walls of abdomen. Do not bloat the abdomen as you breathe in.[33]

Step 2: Fill the *middle* part of the lungs, pushing the lower ribs, breastbone, and chest.

Step 3: Fill the *higher* portion of the lungs, protruding the upper chest, thus lifting chest, upper ribs, expanding region of collar bone.

Step 4: Exhale slowly, holding the chest in firm position, lifting the abdomen upward a little as the air leaves the lungs. When the air is exhaled, relax the chest and abdomen.

Yogic breathing greatly improves your ability to breathe full breaths, expands the lungs, and can elongate your lifespan. "Scientists also claim that just by changing the way we inhale and exhale many of the modern maladies - asthma, anxiety, ADHD, psoriasis, and many more - could either be reduced or reversed."[65]

3.4.5 Chanting Mantra (Repetition)

Just like the breathing meditation, the chanting of Mantra is also a form of yoga, and is known in Indian traditions as

"Mantra yoga". And just like Pranayama, the Mantra yoga is yet another method, another vehicle for transcending the mental disturbances, calming your mind, improving your concentration, and diving deep through the levels of mind (iceberg) to reach a state of deep awareness. "Instead of using the powers of intellect, reasoning, willpower, imagination, or breath, you use the mechanical resource of Mantra."[30] The "Mantra" is nothing but a sound, or more aptly a succession of sounds, which when repeated rhythmically over and over again deepens your consciousness, captures the wandering mind, and keeps your mind anchored into the vibrations of the sound. Each sound in a Mantra has a specific vibrational frequency and rhythm of its own, configured and arranged in a specific pattern which has been time-tested to work for these purposes.

The word "Mantra" consists of two words, 'Man' meaning mind and 'Tri' meaning cross. In Mantra yoga you cross over from mind to no-mind, reaching the realm of silence within. Using the powerful practice of Mantra yoga many seers and yogis of the past were able to cross over to a state of enlightenment. The eastern traditions have hundreds of Mantras, most of which are in Sanskrit language, and many sacred or symbolic in meaning. The chanting of Mantra can be a completely secular activity and there are several mantras (sounds) which are culture-and-tradition--based, not attached to any religion. The ancient Indians, Chinese, Japanese, Hawaiians, Africans, Middle Eastern, Native Americans, Native Australians, and many others, crafted many mantras and prayers, examined the effects of harmony of those sounds with our mental states (thoughts, emotions, feelings), and experienced all powerful benefits of a meditative process.

The chanting and repetition of Mantra is venerable, universal and been validated by millions of men and women of every age, of every religion, to be a powerful and transformative process. From a religious perspective, almost every religion and wisdom tradition advocates for repetition of God's name in some or the other format because the prophets, sages and saints of all ages experienced and understood its great power and glory.[47]

Numerous modern scientific studies have shown that repetition of Mantra, chanting it loudly or silently, reduces symptoms of stress, anxiety and depression and increases positive emotions. Dr. Herbert Benson of Harvard University, in the early 1970s, researched how the chanting of mantras draws the mind into quieter and quieter states, consciously reducing tension throughout your body.

An important aspect about Mantra is that it cannot be translated. The words and sounds in Mantra are like a chemical formula, thoughtfully arranged in a particular order and succession of sounds in order to create a powerful energy connection with practitioner's mind and body. Any translation of the Mantra will result in the alteration of this formula, disrupt its order, and then Mantra will cease to be a Mantra and lose all its power. "It will no longer harmonize the vibrations that enable consciousness to become still. Mantra is therefore unique and untranslatable."[30]

The sound AUM is one of the most popular Mantras across the meditation world, especially with the Indian and Buddhist practitioners (Hindus say AUM, while Tibetans say OM). This sound, however, does not belong to one country or religion. We see variations of AUM in Amen or Ameen which the Christians and Muslims say. Nobody can claim ownership of this sound and it was not invented by anybody. AUM is the symbol for universal frequency and the rhythm of the universe. As per ancient philosophy, AUM represents unity consciousness. In my perspective, the relationship of AUM and consciousness is synonymous to the relationship of "www" and Internet, a common thread, a common symbol, if you will. "Wherever you sit for meditation, in whatever form, you will ultimately end in experiencing AUM or the Hum, the cosmic sound."[47]

AUM includes three primal sounds, Aa + Ou + Mm. The sound Aa comes through the throat, simply by opening your mouth, keeping the tongue rooted, and making a sound. The sound Ou comes through your chest up to the lips. The sound Mm comes through the belly, closing lips. And the vibrations of this combined sound reverberate throughout the body and especially across the regions of your brain, flowing through the Chakras and affecting every cell in your body. From an Eastern philosophical perspective AUM represents the holy trinity where A is creation, U is preservation, and M is culmination.

As covered in the earlier segment, chanting Mantra is one of the six core elements of a wholesome meditation practice. Whatever the form and type of practice, you must include the exercise of chanting Mantra. The core practices of breathing meditation, relaxation techniques and chanting Mantra work in tandem and help practitioners find freedom from an imprisoned mind.

Tips on choosing your Mantra:

If you do not have religious limitations then I'd recommend the beginners to use AUM as your first mantra. You will find scores of resources online on chanting AUM the correct way with correct sound and correct length. You must choose your mantra carefully and thoughtfully as it is something that you will repeat multiple times during your meditation practice. You may choose a mantra that has a religious significance based on your faith or it could be something that is completely secular. For example, a Christian may choose “Ave Maria", a Hindu “Rama Rama”, a Muslim “Allah Hu Akbar”, a Buddhist “Aum”, and a non-believer may choose "Peace " or "Love " or something else.

Most people choose a religious verse, a hymn, a small prayer, a sound that has been repeatedly chosen by many others, and in some sense carries an indescribable power in itself. As mentioned earlier, choose something that is personal and meaningful, based on your faith and preferences. Also, mantras may range from one syllable to a long chant. I suggest that instead of choosing only one short word or two, you choose a Mantra which contains at least a few words. For example, instead of only 'Jesus' or 'Peace', you would rather use 'Jesus, my Lord and my saviour', or instead of OM you may use 'OM shaanti... shaanti...shantihee' (meaning universal peace, peace and peace).

Secondly, the speed at which you chant and repeat your mantra is also an important consideration. Take the following 'loving kindness' mantra as an example.

"May everyone be safe and secure
May everyone be healthy and strong
May everyone be happy and purposeful
May everyone be at peace."

Once you memorize it, you can chant the whole Mantra within 4 seconds, or do it in 6 seconds, or slow it down to 8 seconds, or even 10 seconds. My suggestion is the slower the better.

Some of the popular mantras like "Om Mani Padme Hum", "Sa Ta Na Ma", "AUM", and others are commonly timed around 6 seconds. Also, while you chant your mantra, pay attention to the vibrations in your body, and make sure that your pronunciation, your sound, is correct and clear. In my daily meditation practice I chant the great "Gayatri Mantra" for 108 repetitions, which takes about 12 to 20 minutes to complete one cycle depending upon the speed with which I chant. The Gayatri Mantra is one of the most sacred and powerful mantras available in Indian traditions. Talk to your elders in the house or community, or your guru, some wise person, on how to choose your mantra. That is what I did. The mantra that I chant, most of them, I received from my Guru and my parents. You may have multiple mantras in your arsenal and there is no specific rule of having only one or only two or some fixed number. For beginners I recommend sticking with only one Mantra for the first six months and add more later as you become adept in your meditation practice.

3.4.6. Relaxation

One of the primary objectives of meditation is to relax your mind. The yogic breathing exercises and Mantra repetition produces a calming effect that will relax your mind. There are some other types of practices, however, that are specifically designed to relax both the mind and the body. Just as a good massage will release the tension in your muscles and relax the physical body, the relaxation-oriented meditation practices will release tension on your mind and relax your body. It will help you experience deep calmness and restfulness at both mental and physical levels.

There is a wide variety of relaxation techniques offered in the East and the West among which the "progressive" relaxation practices appear to be more popular and are my personal favourite. Many of the techniques in this category which are similar in nature help relax the whole mind and body, and reduce stress and anxiety. I include two such practices in my "SoZo Meditation" program. In a progressive relaxation exercise, you navigate your attention across each muscle group or each part of your body, moving from one part to another, from head to toe or from toe to head, progressively, in a particular order. You focus your attention on a muscle group, become aware, and in the next instance you withdraw your attention and focus it on to the next muscle group. For example, starting at left toes, you focus your attention on toes for a second, then withdraw instantly to focus it upon the bottom of your feet, and then on to top of your feet, then ankle, and so on.

In another variation of the exercise, you don't just focus and withdraw your attention, but in the instance of your focus you tighten the muscle group, hold it in tight for a few seconds and in the instance of withdrawal you relax the muscle group. And you do it with varying intensity and iterations. These methods have been scientifically proven to relax the mind and body and practiced by millions of people all over the world. A detailed guidance including step-by-step instructions on how to perform these exercises is included in chapter 6.

One of the main applications of this technique is as a sleep aid and is recommended to be practiced before going to bed in order to get a good night's sleep. It is also useful after an intense physical workout or an intense meditation session in order to relax your body. One particular technique popularized in the Western world is the "relaxation response" developed by Harvard cardiologist Dr. Herbert Benson in 1960s.[52] He has documented the various health benefits of using this technique and which includes pain management, fibromyalgia, heart diseases, chronic stress management, and various other physiological and neurological disorders. Practicing meditation and relaxation activates the parasympathetic nervous system which quiets the nerves, and triggers relaxation response that is associated with the prevention of stress related diseases.

In the "progressive" relaxation techniques you navigate your attention and awareness around each muscle group in your whole body, from head to toe, progressively, one after another. You either tighten and relax the muscle group as you navigate, or within a split second you focus and withdraw your attention on each muscle group as you navigate. These methods have been scientifically proven to relax the mind and the body and are practiced by millions all over the world including professional athletes, gymnasts, and meditators.

Lastly, it only takes about 3 to 5 minutes to perform the two relaxation exercises included in the “SoZo Meditation” program. And the effects of the exercise are simply magical. The great sense of relief and relaxation that one may experience at the end of the workout might pleasantly surprise a beginner. You will feel lighter, relaxed and re-energized. Your sleep will get better with regular practice. The core practices of yogic breathing, chanting mantra, and relaxation exercises work collectively as a whole and lead the practitioner into the silence within.

Before we move on to the next segment, let us recap the 6 core elements of meditation practice:

1. Intention and Faith
2. Concentration and Awareness
3. Sitting Posture (Attitude)

4. Breath Mastery (Focus)
5. Chanting Mantra (Repetition)
6. Relaxation

All the six core elements of meditation covered in this segment are beautifully summarized in the poetry below.

"In a fair, still spot

Having fixed his abode- not too much raised,

Nor yet too low- let him abide, his goods

a cloth, a deerskin, and the Kusha-grass.

There, setting hard his mind upon the One,

Restraining heart and senses, silent, calm,

let him accomplish *Yoga*, and achieve

Pureness of soul, holding immovable

body and neck and head, his gaze absorbed

Upon his nose-end, rapt from all around,

Tranquil in spirit, free of fear, intent

Upon his *Brahmacharya* vow, devout

musing on Me, lost in me thought of Me."[40]

CHAPTER 4
THE BEST-PRACTICES OF MEDITATION PRACTICE

4.1 - Time, Place, And Duration (When, Where, How Long to Practice)

In this segment, I address in a very straightforward way some of the most basic questions about practicing meditation: What's the best time to meditate? Is the place important? How long is long enough? These three aspects, although seemingly simple considerations, are perhaps the most important practical elements of any good meditation-practice.

These are the fundamental building blocks of a disciplined practice. Without discipline there is no progress, and without progress you cannot realize the many benefits of practicing meditation.

Waking up early in the morning to meditate in your nicely decorated meditation room, with soothing aromas of incense burning, tranquil music playing in the background, dim lights, and meditation cushions- all that should not be just a one-day feel-good affair or a show off. Discipline comes from repetition, doing what you intend to do every single day, day in and day out, without fail, with a deep commitment, and with your eyes on the ultimate goal.

In addition to providing answers to the basic questions about the time, place, and duration I list down some of the best practices and key considerations for practicing meditation. These critical insights will help you continue your meditation journey for a long haul.

1. WHEN to meditate?

Morning time is generally considered to be the best time for meditation. However, if the mornings are busy for you then you may choose any time during the day when you are free and able to dedicate a few minutes for your meditation practice. Please make sure you do not have to be somewhere else immediately after finishing your practice - an appointment, a pre-commitment, or a deadline pressing on your mind. No point rushing your meditation practice when your mind is under time pressure.

The primary objective here is to relax your mind and body and de-stress, not rush. If you are pressed for time, or you are expecting to be busy in the immediate future then find another time-slot sometime later in the day. First, get done with your commitments and priorities related to work, daily chores, attending to kids, the drive to the grocery store, cooking, watching your favourite show on TV, and so on. Simply put, give meditation your priority after all other priorities are taken care of. This way, as a beginner, when you sit for meditation, there would be nothing else waiting for you, nothing else to attend to, and you will be able to focus better on your practice. When you become adept in meditation and experience its amazing benefits, you will be motivated to put meditation first and everything else second.

Early mornings are not suitable for all. Let's talk about working professionals - folks who have to start their day at 5 am. They have to make breakfast, get the kids ready for school, get themselves ready, finish daily chores, dress up, make up, walk the dog, drive to office, catch a train and so on; for them, finding even one extra minute in the morning for anything else is an absolute impossibility. There is no point trying to somehow squeeze in a meditation session into a packed morning schedule.

For such people, my recommendation, and based on my personal experience, is to pick a time around 12 noon, just before your lunch break and practice your daily "SoZo Meditation". I would get a 30-minute lunch break at my office sometime between 11:30 and 12:30. In my small private office I'd roll down a yoga mat on the floor beside my desk, and stick a note on the door that said "12-Minute Meditation in progress. Knock if urgent. Thanks!".

The point is that if you have a genuine intent of getting something done then you will find ways to make it happen. As it's said popularly, "Where there is a will there's a way".

On the other hand, if your mornings are a little easy and you are not pressed for time then it is best to practice meditation before breakfast. If that's a little tough, then how about an hour after breakfast? That works too. As a thumb rule, practice on an empty stomach, either before meals, or sixty to ninety minutes after. And ideally, you must strive to maintain a fixed-time, fixed-place routine for your practice as doing so cultivates discipline. OSHO says "Cleanse your mind twice, morning and evening, and you will see tremendous positive change."

2. WHERE to meditate?

It's simple. Whatever place you pick, firstly make sure that it is clean and hygienic. And secondly, make sure you have as few distractions around you as possible. Avoid places with disturbances or loud noises. Ideally, find a secluded spot where you can be alone for some time. If you have people around walking, talking, or kids playing around, or loud TV and music, or other distracting sights and sounds and smells, then your practice will become harder and ineffective.

It is therefore important that you find a quiet and clean space - be it indoors, outdoors, a cozy corner in your home, a small meditation room, or in your backyard, in the park, under a tree, in your office, in a place of worship, at a yoga centre, a gym, a mountain, or any other place of your choice. Again, try to maintain a fixed-time fixed-place routine as much as possible.

3. HOW LONG to meditate?

You do not have to sit for long hours in meditation and as such, there is no standard rule about the duration of practice. The duration is highly variable based upon the type and the form of practice, the elements contained within the practice, and the practitioner's personal goals, capacity and preference. The monks, yogis, and advanced practitioners might practice meditation for several hours each day. Some others might do it for an hour or two each day, or for thirty-minutes twice a week, and so on. There is no right or wrong number for the duration of your practice. It is dependent upon a lot of factors, and mainly on the spare time you have in your super-busy lives.

For a beginner or for anyone struggling with time, I recommend starting with 12-minute "SoZo Meditation" once daily. That's it. Everybody on the planet, however busy you are, whatever you do in life, wherever you are, you always have 12 minutes of free time that can be devoted to something as important as meditation-practice. You may gradually, over time, increase the duration to 15 minutes, 20 minutes, 30 minutes, and so on.

I strongly recommend beginners to stick to the 12-minute practice for at least the first six months, and then increase the duration as you make progress. If you want to get more done in a day, you may consider doing two twelve-minute "SoZo Meditation" sessions per day, one in the morning and one in the evening.

Each person progresses differently and at a different pace. There is no competition or comparison. You assess your own progress and determine if you are ready for longer practice. Feel free to experiment. Don't be scared. Whatever the duration of your practice, make sure to apply all the ground rules (covered in chapter 6) one hundred percent without cutting corners. Also be wary of the techniques and forms that promise faster results or miraculous effects. Real progress takes time and there is nothing wrong about it.[48]

And lastly, you must strive to maintain a fixed-time, fixed-place routine for your practice as doing so cultivates discipline. We are not going to always feel like meditating but the important thing is to put some time into it.

4.2 - Key Considerations And Long-haul Strategy

Once upon a time at a Vedic Gurukul (school) in ancient India, an apparently frustrated disciple goes to his master and says, "Master, I have been meditating diligently for months and for several hours each day. I do all my spiritual exercises and say my prayers every day. Why then in spite of all my hard work and commitment I cannot see God and experience enlightenment?" The master calmly takes note of his disciple's complaints and asks the disciple to meet him by the lake the next morning.

When the disciple arrives as instructed, the master asks him to take a plunge in the water. As soon as the disciple dives beneath the surface, the master holds him underwater with force for over a minute and doesn't let him out. The disciple finally pulls himself out, frantically gasping for air, bewildered, and asks his guru, "Why, master? Why would you do this to me?"

The master replies, "The urge with which you sought air to breathe right now, if you can show the same urge in your meditation practice, only then will you meet the Creator". The disciple was enlightened at that very moment.

Humans are impatient by nature and we want instant results. Our culture places tremendous emphasis on instant gratification and quick fixes. We are busy people and we do not have time for things that take time. I once came across an advertisement by a US-based Psychic that said something like "Remove all mental clouds for $1 per minute and find enlightenment". Some other advertisement said something like "Become a Buddha in 30 minutes meditation for only $19.99". This means that what took prince Siddhartha Gautama eight years to achieve and become a Buddha, can be yours in a mere

30 minutes. Unfortunately, many people fall into such bogus traps.

The reality is that skills develop through long periods of striving. Learning to love the plateau where nothing seems to be happening and continuing to repeat the routine day in and day out is an essential mental disciple.[42] Achieving anything meaningful is a marathon, not a sprint. It requires persistence, discipline and a steady state of energy that lasts over time. Patanjali, the author of Yoga Sutras, says, "Progress comes swiftly to those who try their hardest".

Perform your practice with sincere intent and mindfulness. The zen master Thich Nhat Hanh said, "When doing the dishes, do the dishes." The same way, when doing meditation, do the meditation. Be fully engaged. Be fully engrossed. Be happy about what you are doing and give your one hundred percent attention to the activity at hand. Mindfulness is nothing but that.

Sitting cross-legged with eyes closed most beginners might feel like fools to be just sitting and doing nothing. When you first start meditating you notice how active your mind is and you may feel agitated and helpless. The thoughts of various kinds flood your consciousness and you are unable to control the monkey-mind. There is also physical discomfort sitting in one place.

"As a beginner, initially you may feel that nothing is happening and this practice cannot possibly be useful. You are not alone. The process of meditation can be slow, and the changes that occur are subtle and unfold over time."[18] Our minds are filled with alternative activities that are more enjoyable or useful than sitting still and breathing. Yet, learning how to remain engaged in our lives even with the feelings of boredom can be a valuable experience.

A surfer who finds paddling to be boring and is interested only in catching the wave will never be able to surf. In order to experience that exuberance and excitement of riding a big wave, the surfer must learn to love paddling first.

Most beginners ask me the same kind of questions, like – "How long would it take for me to experience the benefits of meditation?" or, "How soon will I be able to calm my restless mind? or How soon can I get relief from my stress and anxiety?" and so on. It is quite normal to have these questions, and it is synonymous in a way to asking the doctor how soon you will feel better after starting the prescribed medication.

With meditation practice, it is quite possible that you will experience reduction in anxiety and stress perhaps instantly, within the first few minutes of your first session. The measurable and significant benefits that are long-lasting, however, accrue with regular practice over a period of 4 to 8 weeks. And this time-range is also a good baseline for you to measure your progress and assess your success with meditation-practice.

Avoid being judgmental and critical about your performance. Go easy on yourself. Everything gets better with regular practice, and that takes time and discipline. You don't need to seek external validation or experiential learnings from outside. At the end of the day, it is your experience that counts.[42] A great trumpet player, Miles Davis, once said, "Sometimes you have to play for a long time before you can play like yourself".[18]

Lastly, I would reiterate that it is vital for you to maintain a fixed time, place and routine for your daily practice. This will train your mind in converting the practice into a daily habit. Once the habit is formed you will be on auto-pilot mode, self-motivated, and you won't have to be reminded or forced to practice. If, for some reason, you cannot maintain a fixed time and place, don't sweat, and don't beat yourself up. Just do your meditation whenever you find free time, which could be late evening, late night, early morning, whenever. As long as you get your daily dose of meditation you are good, you are making progress.

4.3 - Birth Of "SoZo Meditation": A 12-Minute Scalable Technique and Program

In this section I explain what "SoZo Meditation" is all about and what inspired me to create this unique program. I am not claiming that "SoZo Meditation" is a unique concept in terms of duration only. There are tons of time-based techniques and programs out there: 5-minute meditation, 10-minute meditation, 30-minute meditation, all the way to 60 minute and longer versions. The SoZo Meditation is unique from the *combined* perspective of simplicity, scalability, efficiency, practicality, duration, content, and the ease of application into daily life of modern humans.

In order to understand the real meaning behind "SoZo Meditation" let us first take a quick look at some of the common concerns most beginners have about practicing meditation -

"I am so busy that I cannot find an extra 30 minutes for meditation."

"I am so stressed out that I cannot focus on anything."

"I cannot stop thinking. My mind is flooded with thoughts as I close my eyes to meditate."

"I don't have patience to sit cross-legged in one place and meditate."

"I cannot imagine not checking my phone every few minutes."

"It's easier to workout at the gym than to meditate."

"Is meditation practice scientific?"

If you look closely at these concerns, you will notice people are actually relaying the very problems the meditation can help resolve - stress, anxiety, impatience, the lack of focus, inability to concentrate, incessant thinking, and so on. Sadly, this also reflects a serious lack of awareness and education about what mediation is really about with its immense benefits for mental and emotional health.

Our lives are undoubtedly busy, and our attention span has worsened over the years. We struggle to focus upon one thing and deeply immerse ourselves into something for more than a few seconds at a time. Our attention has caught monkey-mind syndrome, jumping from one thought to another, from one activity to another, and in modern times from one screen to another. Our priorities and interests have changed a great deal in the 21st century as we are trying to squeeze more and more things into less and less time.

We belong to a time in history where people worship relentless pace and a speed that'd bring even Alexander the Great to his knees. Therefore, in respect to the duration of practice in particular, what worked decades ago is not going to work in this day and age.

Any practice spanning hours- or for that matter even thirty-minutes long- might be impractical and discouraging in today's times. Even when the 'run Forrest run' level of urgency is realized, and the wide-ranging benefits of meditation practice explained, there will still be resistance. The practice needs to be practical enough from a time-duration perspective and must fit into our daily routine.

This got me thinking-

(a) How do I address and resolve the 'Duration issue'? (b) What could be done to make the practice more practical and attractive enough for beginners? and (c) What is the magic formula, other than increased knowledge and awareness, to successfully motivate people for meditation? Would a new type or form or technique of meditation work? But there already are thousands of varieties out there. Would a new customized program work? But there are already thousands of programs and offerings in the market.

It quickly became clear to me that in order to find a solution I must find ways to trim down the duration and conceptualize a shorter version of meditation-practice. And I needed to do this without sacrificing its fundamental functionality and efficiency. Well, I found a solution in my favourite sport - Cricket!

The game of Cricket is quite popular in England and its former colonies - India, Australia, South Africa, New Zealand, West Indies, Sri Lanka, Pakistan, and many other countries. The International Cricket Council (ICC) is the governing entity of the sport, and also one of the richest sporting bodies in the world.

Traditionally, for over a century, there were two popular formats of the game - one was 'Test Cricket' and the other was 'One-day Cricket'. Test cricket is played over five days with 8 hours of play each day, whereas the one-day game is played over a day with 8 hours of game and a limited 50 overs bowled by each side.

At the turn of the 21st century, the ICC board and big sponsors of the game noticed less and less crowds turning up for games at the stadium. The television audience too was going down, and so was the revenue.

As people's lives became more and more busy, and with the advent of digital revolution, internet, social media, and communication, the existing formats rendered themselves somewhat obsolete and impractical from a time-duration perspective for modern times. So, the ICC introduced a new format, a shorter version of the game, called 'T20 Cricket', where the entire game duration is about 4 hours long, same as that of an American football game.

The core functionality and the ground rules all remained the same as the previous formats, and only the duration of the game was reduced - by reducing the number of overs bowled from 50 per side to 20 per side (a factor of 2.5). Today the T20 format is successful, profitable, and more importantly, very practical for all the stakeholders in the game, including the ICC, sponsors, viewers and players.

Inspired by this story in my quest to figure out a way to make meditation more appealing and more practical, I designed a shorter version of practice by trimming down the commonly popular 30-minute practice to a 12-minute practice (same factor of 2.5). Twelve minutes is neither too long nor too short. It is that magic number in the middle, perfect for a beginner and for busy people.

From a philosophical and spiritual perspective there is a certain significance of the number 12. The Astral system of the human body is believed to have 12 inner constellations, revolving around the Sun of the omniscient spiritual eye, and is interconnected with the physical sun and the 12 Zodiac signs. The solar cycle is a period of 4356 days, which is approximately 12 years. The ancient *rishis* (wise men) also discovered that man's earthly and heavenly environment occurs in 12-year cycles and pushes him forward on his natural path.

From a scientific perspective, there is one particular research study conducted at the University of Pennsylvania Center for

Spirituality and Mind, including among other things, the 12-minute Kirtan-Kriya (a very specific form of meditation). The study found that the subjects of the research experienced significant and measurable benefits of lowered stress and anxiety levels, and improved brain and memory functioning over a 2-month period of practicing this meditation.[1]

Furthermore, the Chinese healing method of "Acupuncture" is based upon the 12 meridians or pathways or channels that act as conduits for the "Chi" (Prana, Life-force) to flow through various parts of the body, to animate and nourish.

All of the above inspired me to create the "SoZo Meditation" which is a 12-Minute Scalable Technique and Program.

The word "SoZo" is a Greek word which collectively means "save, heal and deliver" (ref. Freedom Tools, by Andy Reese). Biblically, it refers to the spiritual process of inner healing and inner freedom. I was instantly attracted to the word and its meaning touched my heart. SoZo fits perfectly well with my personal story, my personal experience of meditation and its transformative powers. Meditation saved my life, brought healing and recovery, and delivered me onto a path of purpose and spiritual maturity.

Not just that, but SoZo also fits tightly with the core definition of meditation coined by Patanjali, as Chitta Vrutti Nirodha, which essentially means the freedom from mental disturbances (save), reaching a state of lasting peace, joy, compassion and love (heal), and cross-over to your true nature (deliver). Simply enough, I could not think of a better word to name my creation but "SoZo Meditation".

The key features of "SoZo Meditation" are- practicality, simplicity, the content, scalability, flexibility and customization. In its basic form, "SoZo Meditation" is a 12 Minute technique. I include the word "Scalable" in its definition because as you grow in meditation and are able to practice for longer duration sessions, you could then easily scale-up the base program to match your new requirements. I elaborate upon this aspect by providing specific examples in chapter 7. Here's a quick example of the 12-Minute "SoZo Meditation" technique.

DURATION YOU PERFORM

1 minute Setting intention exercise

4 minutes Slow and deep breathing exercise

3 minutes Fast and shallow breathing exercise

4 minutes Chanting Mantra exercise

12 minutes total

The "SoZo Meditation" technique and program is, hands down, all you need to begin your meditation journey in the best possible way.

Lastly, I mentioned earlier that there is a wide variety of forms and types of meditation-practices available to choose from, ranging from “simple, basic and less intense” to “complex, advanced and more intense” styles. As you grow in meditation your practice naturally evolves towards more complex forms like advanced mindfulness practices, Vipassana, TM or other intense breathing yoga workouts.

The main advantage of “SoZo Meditation” and the way it fits into a larger picture is that it acts as a common foundation upon which any of the advanced practices can be built. Think of it as a foundational practice where you develop the qualities of focus, concentration, patience, persistence, posture control, breath control and repetition, and which could be effectively applied in learning some of the more advanced forms.

4.4 - The Secret Formula to Success with Meditation

"Only you can take inner freedom from yourself, or give it to yourself. Nobody else can." from the book Untethered Soul by Michael A. Singer

In order to find out the answers to questions like - Whether or not meditation is for you? Whether or not it would work for you? Whether or not you will like it? Whether or not you will experience the promised benefits? Whether or not you will be successful? - there is one easy way to figure that out. And I share with you in this segment the secret formula for your success with meditation-practice.

My advice and my formula for all new seekers is to try "SoZo Meditation" for 30 days without quitting. Do it for 30 days without prejudice, without judgments, without having any doubts, without complaining and without making any excuses. All you need is to set aside 12 minutes each day for meditation. You must find a fixed time and place during the day, without fail, for practicing "SoZo Meditation" for 30 days. It is not a big ask at all.

The 12 minutes x 30 days equals 6 hours total in the whole month. That's it. And something as powerful as meditation, with the potential to transform your life positively, deserves to be allotted 6 hours of your time, at the very least. If you are serious about your own healing, about finding ways to lower your stress and anxiety, about stopping the incessant cycle of past-future thinking, then I am sure you will be willing to invest 6 short hours over a month to perform this experiment.

Do it for 30 days and then decide if you want to continue further depending upon whether or not you see the results for yourself.

Be your own witness. Experience for yourself and decide for yourself- Do you feel lighter, as if weight has been lifted off your mind? Do you feel better after meditating? Do you feel more at peace and in control? Has your stress and anxiety gone down? Do you feel the silence and calmness within? These changes are subtle at times, may show up early or may show up later. They are sure to come, though.

Your job is to get to the end no matter what and decide to continue or quit at that point, not any sooner. Do not quit before the 30th day. Commit yourself to completing 30 days and don't give up in the middle. Put meditation first and everything else second. If you are successful in doing this exercise, then in all likelihood, you will experience several of the listed benefits of meditation practice and you will be ready to continue beyond 30 days, pursuing meditation for the rest of your life. I am quite certain that at the end of your 30-day experiment, you will find great relief from the mental disturbances that have been causing restlessness, and you will experience a sense of calm and peace.

Lastly, don't expect every day to be a triumph. Some days will be hard. In reality, the healing journey is full of stumbles and backtracking before a big leap forward. Keep at it with patience and confidence, and soon enough you will join the league of millions of others whose life is positively transformed by practicing medittion.

CHAPTER 5
RELATIONSHIP - MEDITATION WITH RELIGION & SPIRITUALITY

The history of religion and spirituality is thousands of years old and the libraries around the world are filled with countless books and scriptures on these subjects. There is really nothing new I can tell you about this matter. However, when it comes to the relationship between meditation and religion, and between meditation and spirituality, I believe I have some important things to clarify for my readers. Unfortunately, there are some deep-rooted misconceptions about this topic, and these wrongly held views and opinions in turn block many from pursuing meditation. In this segment, I provide authentic insights, in a concise manner, which will disprove some of the prevalent myths around practicing meditation as it relates to religion and spirituality.

I am cognizant of the fact that talking about religion and spirituality could turn into a sensitive matter due to some strongly held beliefs, un-beliefs, and intolerance, and therefore, I cautiously and consciously limit the scope of the discussion in this segment. I shall, only very briefly, touch upon this subject, and do that purely from the perspective of establishing the relationship of meditation with religion and spirituality.

The fact is that meditation and meditation-practice by itself is not a religious or a spiritual exercise. In spite of its origins in ancient philosophical systems closely linked with Hinduism and its growth in Buddhist traditions, the meditation practice is in all practicality a secular and universal phenomenon. At the same time, however, any form of meditation could potentially be converted into a religious or spiritual activity if the practitioner chooses to do so. Every practitioner has a complete freedom to incorporate religious aspects into one's own meditation-practice based on their religious beliefs, preferences and personal goals. I will elaborate on this "personalization" aspect which is at the core of the relationship between meditation and spirituality, and I do it in a succinct manner.

5.1 - Freedom to Integrate Religion

Meditation in itself really has nothing to do with any religion, and its practice is not a religious activity in any particular form. Meditation did originate in India's ancient philosophical systems; however, it is neither attached to a particular creed or cult or religion, nor is it patented for use by only a specific group of people. Meditation asks for no change of beliefs and does not belong to any movement.

Millions of people around the world belonging to various different religions, nationality, cultures and ethnicities, all practice meditation in a universal way without any limitations or restrictions, whatsoever. The Hindus, Christians, Jews, Buddhists, Muslims, Sikhs, Parsis, Taoists, Atheists, Agnostics, Whites, Blacks, Browns, Asians, Hispanics, Natives, Men, Women, LGBTQ, Young, Old – ALL are welcome with open arms to practice mediation without restrictions and without any qualifying criteria. The way I see it, meditation is an open system, much like today's internet – free to use and explore by every human being on the planet, irrespective of any particular form of categorization and labelling enforced by society.

By virtue of being an open system, the practitioner has freedom to integrate religious elements into his or her own meditation practice. This means that the practice can be personalized as per your individual faith and personal preferences. For example, in a focused attention exercise, you may choose your object of attention to be your God or an Angel or some religious symbol – a cross, star, moon, an idol, or a passage from a sacred text, say. Similarly, in the exercise of chanting Mantra, a Christian may chant "Jesus Jesus", a Muslim 'Allah Hu

Akbar", a Hindu 'Om Namah Shivaya', a Jew "Shalom Shalom", a Buddhist "Nam Myoho Renge Kyo', and so on.

In their book "How God Changes Your Brain" authors Andrew Newberg and Robert Waldman note that the Bible has over twenty references to meditation. "In Genesis, Isaac went to meditate in the field. In Joshua, the followers were commanded by law to meditate night and day. The reference to meditation can be found in all these passages – Genesis 24:63, Joshua 1:8, PSALM (1:2, 5:1, 19:4, 49:3, 63:6, 77:12, 104:34, 119:115, 119:46, 119:78, 119:97, 119:99, 119:148, 143:5, Isaiah 33:18, Luke 21:14, Timothy 4:115, and Matthew 7:13). In the 12th century, Guigo II, a Carthusian monk categorized four levels of meditation practice – Lectio (slow reading of a Bible passage), Meditio (pondering deeper meaning), Oratio (prayer), and Contemplato (wordless focus on God's Love). In the 10th century, St. Ignatius developed a series of spiritual meditation exercises."[1]

In the Bhagavad Gita, the five-thousand-year-old quintessential religious document of the Hindus, the Lord of the Lords 'Sri Krishna' prescribes four different yoga-paths (ways of life) that one can follow to cultivate a life of purpose and enlightenment: (1) Karma-Yog (path of action), (2) Gyan-Yog (path of knowledge), (3) Bhakti-Yog (path of devotion), and (4) Raj-Yog (path of meditation). In verses 6.46 and 8.28 of the Gita, Krishna nominates the path of meditation, the Raj-Yog, to be the most supreme path of the four. In verse 5.27 and 5.28 Krishna talks about meditation and yogic-breathing as the way the wise master their mind, senses and intellect. Ignoring such profound guidance from sacred scriptures on the great powers of meditation would be, quite frankly, a missed opportunity for our real freedom.

Practitioners in every religious tradition have succeeded in reaching the mystical states and the deeper states of consciousness. The fact is that, meditation-practice cultivates a deeper awareness, a deeper compassion, which in turn has the power to dissolve the differences and divisions of race, religion, and identity between human beings. By bringing down the walls of personality the meditation practice cultivates a feeling of love towards each other and for everything else in the universe.

The expanded awareness develops greater acceptance for other people's religious beliefs. "Love Thy Neighbour as yourself," said Jesus. Through meditation we discover that underneath our mortal bodies everybody is connected to the same eternal soul, the same spirit within. And then when you realize this truth, you experience eternal peace and happiness.

This eternity principle brings us to the doorstep of spirituality and its relationship with meditation, and which I cover in the next section.

5.2 - Life is Spiritual by Nature

"All problems are psychological, but all solutions are spiritual."

- Thomas Hara, MD

Spirituality is a term broadly describing the personal pursuit of the reality that resides within us. We are all spiritual beings by nature. Down the centuries for millennia the spiritual teachers have told us that our life is a spiritual journey, and we are moving through births and deaths towards real freedom, to experience life beyond limitations. It is a journey towards the inner realm within us which is called by different names like – God, higher power, eternal spirit, a higher state of consciousness, the One, Thee, Thou, the universe within, the higher mind, and so on. And the purpose of this inner pursuit is to discover and experience the innate qualities of the inner realm, that of eternal peace, joy, and wisdom.

Whether you know it or not, we all seek a higher power. The longing manifests in many ways – our desire to heal; our desire to belong; our drive to know our purpose in life; the urge to escape the limitations of the sensory world; or our desire for transcendent experience. Spirituality is therefore your personal quest to connect with your inner self, with a universal energy that pervades everything in the cosmos, and touch base with the real purpose of your life on earth which is often defined as the 'journey back to the maker'.

When many people think of spirituality, they automatically think of organized religion. There is a big difference between practicing religion and becoming spiritually aware. Religion is created by man. Religion is a dogma, a prescribed set of beliefs, rituals, moral commandments, and practices. Every religion tends to think that its way is the way. But spirituality does not have any such distinction and differences. It is inclusive and universal. You may or may not be religious, that is your choice. But spirituality is not a choice. Life itself is spiritual, and spirituality is at the center of everything we do and everything we are.

Furthermore, a spiritual experience can be defined in both religious and secular terms. Religion is one of the many paths available to us for our spiritual journey. A believer may see God as a multitude of ideas, images, symbols, feelings, sensations, or in the form of a personal relationship like a friend, father, guide, teacher, mother, creator, judge, lawgiver, miracle worker, or a distant observer of humanity's fate. A non-believer on the other hand may see the unknown as some higher power, as a matrix, or a spirit in the heartland within.

The earthly cycle of birth and death is not all there is to life. "Unlike the body that disintegrates after death, the spirit is eternal and never dies" is the central concept of many spiritual and religious traditions. In the East it is believed that the spirit moves on from one birth to another, the reincarnation principle, and that your good and bad karma along with your spiritual maturity gets carried forward into the next life. And once all of your karmic debt is paid off you are released from the cycle of birth-death and you attain: Moksha, Nirvana, Samadhi, Enlightenment, Liberation.

The central premise of spirituality as defined in ancient scriptures is that there are two modes of existence: one the individual soul (lower-mind, Jiva) and other one the universal-soul (higher-mind, Atman). The concept is in a way similar to the Samkhya philosophy covered in Chapter-3. The individual soul is changeable, conditioned, transitory, ego-driven, a bundle of personality, thoughts, emotions, memories, and sense perceptions. While the universal soul is unchangeable, unconditioned, eternal and formless. And it is our identification with the individual-soul, lower mind, that is the reason for all human suffering. To be able to find real happiness and peace you must first disidentify with the lower-mind and identify with the higher-mind, which tends to be obscured behind the walls of the conditioned mind, like the sun hidden behind dark clouds.

In meditation, when the mind is silenced and consciousness deepened, you are able to touch upon your Atman (the higher-mind), the deeper core that is there when you strip away all the personality, race, gender, the whole identity. "Meditation creates a conducive internal environment in order to release the grasp of self-identity and ego on the mind, and that is the only way you escape your mind's prison to discover true freedom, peace and healing."[21]

One of the greatest cultural differences between the East and the West is that pursuing meditative and spiritual practices as a cure for the mind's self-inflicted problems of stress, anxiety, fear and so on, is a normal goal in life in the East.[2] Developing consciousness and having mental control are considered great spiritual pursuits in Eastern traditions. And in the traditional meditation practice of Pranayama it all begins with 'breath'. This is why yogic-breathing is often considered a spiritual exercise. Author Deepak Chopra says, "In meditation, the Yogi (one who is adept in meditation, the meditator) tries to clear the path for feelings, emotions, thoughts, and all mental disturbances of his mind, so that he can actually experience the bedrock of inner satisfaction that all the ancient scriptures declared to be our birthright."

In Bhagavad Gita, Lord Krishna educates his disciple Arjuna, the great warrior, that every person shelters a dweller in the body who is wholly unlike the isolated and vulnerable ego and ever-changing personality, and describes this Inner Self as follows:[2]

> *"Weapons cannot cleave him Fire cannot burn him Water cannot wet him Wind cannot dry him He is eternal and all-pervading Subtle, immovable, and ever the same."*

Spirituality is all about connecting with your true nature where there is an abundance of peace, joy, wisdom, happiness, love and healing. And one of the pathways to reach this place is that of meditation practice.

CHAPTER 6
PRACTICAL GUIDE - WHAT TO DO? AND HOW TO DO?

6.1 - A Simple, Thoughtful, And Practical 5-step Approach

This is your daily practice which covers the 'what to do' and 'how to do' of meditation practice. It really does not get any easier than this, I promise. Using my years of experience practicing meditation and with an aim of creating something simple yet practical for a beginner living a busy life, I have created a well-thought-out "SoZo Meditation" program. This simple technique will help you begin your meditation journey in a most effective manner. As I noted once before that I am a mere middleman, a beggar showing other beggars where and how I found bread. I am excited to share my knowledge and insights from my personal experience and provide beginners with the right tools and guidance in practicing meditation.

I can point you in the right direction- however, the journey is yours to take.

At the very beginning of the book, I mentioned -not hundreds of confusing practices; not thousands of confusing forms and types, but only a handful of the most fundamental techniques are included in this book. That's all you really need as a beginner: simple meditation exercises and a simple program that can be implemented in your daily busy life with ease. Meditation is not about looking for some special experience like a celebrity weekend-yoga retreat or similar. It is a daily and disciplined practice which simply asks you to breathe the right way and unburden your mind. It asks you to simply connect with the present moment fully and look within.

My mantra for beginners is "Do Less, Achieve More" and "Simplify". And that is the kind of approach I prescribe in this book. In doing less, however, there is no cutting-the-corners mentality. There is no taking shortcuts. In fact, it is the opposite. "SoZo Meditation" program includes a select few exercises which cover all the six core elements of meditation-practice - intention and faith, concentration, yogic breathing, repetition, posture, and relaxation.

I have carefully designed a 5-step approach for an aspirant of meditation to follow. And I strongly recommend you review each section with full attention and follow the instructions to the end. If you are serious about getting onboard with meditation, I suggest you be earnest and sincere in your pursuit. Don't rush. Slow down and absorb everything in this chapter. One step at a time. Adopt a beginner's mentality. Be eager to learn.

If you think you already know better, then you will probably not benefit from what I have to say. If you miss learning and implementing the ground rules of practice as described here then your practice will not only be faulty and ineffective but it may also have adverse effects on your respiratory and nervous system.

The content in this section may appear to be a bit lengthy- however, that is because I provide a detailed, step-by-step instructions, for each meditation exercise included in my program, covering the finer aspects, tips, cautions, and the best practices. I wish I had received this level of guidance when I started my meditation practice as it'd help me avoid the common mistakes that most beginners struggle to overcome. My unique approach here, I promise, will fast-track your progress.

Your life is going to change and you are going to experience great calmness and peace of mind. You will be happier than before. You will have more energy than before. Your outlook towards life will be more positive. Your relationship with your spouse, kids, family, friends and work colleagues is going to blossom and get deeper. You will cruise through your day with more ease and tranquillity. Your intuition will become stronger. You will be able to face the various problems of your life with greater control and mindfulness. Shed all your doubts and begin your practice with confidence and excitement.

The 5-Step Approach

Step 1 (section 6.2)

This will take only 5 minutes of your time where we will experiment with different types of breathing. This is for you to get the feel of things.

Step 2 (section 6.3 and 6.4)

I lay down the massively important Ground Rules that must be followed in your daily practice. I encourage you to read it, re-read it, re-re-read it, and learn it by heart.

Step 3 (section 6.5)

I prescribe and list 5 Yogic Breathing Exercises that will be included in your "SoZo Meditation" practice and "SoZo Meditation" program. And I include detailed step-by-step instructions on how to perform each exercise.

Step 4 (section 6.6)

I prescribe and detail out two Relaxation Techniques which are included in your "SoZo Meditation" program. And I include the step-by-step instructions on how to perform each exercise.

Step 5 (section 7.2 and 7.3)

I prescribe the "SoZo Meditation" program. This program is your main guide. The program is your game plan for the first 30 days, then next 60 days, then next 90 days and beyond. The program includes exactly what you will do, in what sequence and for how long.

6.2 - Experiment with Breath (Step 1/5)

This experiment will take only about FIVE minutes of your time to complete and I urge my readers, especially the beginners, not to skip this part. This experiment is like a trailer before the movie. Or think of it as a wine-tasting exercise, if you will, where you sample different type of wines like Merlot, Zinfandel, Cabernet Sauvignon, Pinot Noir, and so on. In this short and easy experiment, you will modulate your breath, and practice a few different ways of breathing in meditation. You will change the pace, depth, texture, sound, style and rhythm of your breath.

The main objective here is to turn the unconscious process of breathing into a conscious act. You pay attention to your breath, hear it, feel it, and be with it. You also become aware of the various sensations that arise in your body and mind as you breathe.

Do not try to analyze anything at this point. Shed all doubts. We are not pursuing perfection. This is a simple experiment to enhance our understanding of the way we breathe and anchor your attention in meditation. Focus upon completing the experiment without prejudice. Just observe and become aware of what you feel and how you feel during breathing. Watch your breath, hear it, feel it, and be with it.

Key Points:

1. There are twelve short exercises in this experiment which would take about 5 minutes to complete.
2. In each step you will perform 3 breath cycles, which means, you will inhale-exhale 3 times.

<Breathe-in, Breathe-out> <Breathe-in, Breathe-out> <Breathe-in, Breathe-out>

Cycle 1 Cycle 2 Cycle 3

Simple!

3. You must breathe in and breathe out via your nose, not mouth.
4. When you inhale, inhale fully, filling up your lungs to the brim. Don't strain too hard, though. And do not bloat the belly as you inhale, unless specifically instructed to do so.
5. When you exhale, exhale fully, to the point where you feel a little contraction in your belly, and which is a sign that all the air is out of your system.

To begin the experiment, you must take a comfortable posture. Find a clean and quiet spot and sit on a yoga mat or a carpet with your legs crossed. If sitting cross legged is tough then you may choose to sit on a chair or a stool. Just make sure you sit straight; your spine, neck and head are in a straight line. Place your palms on your lap, facing up, left on left and right on right. Relax your body. Release any tension in your body. Be at ease.

There is nothing urgent calling your attention for the next 5 minutes. You have nowhere else to be. Relax. Perform each step of the experiment in sequence, one by one, without skipping. This is a simple and easy exercise and importantly, this is your entry into the world of meditation, joining millions of others who have discovered inner silence. Proceed with a positive attitude and confidence.

Repeat this process for all exercises:

a) Read instructions, b) Gently close your eyes, and c) Perform the exercise.

Begin the experiment.

Exercise #1

Breathe slowly and deeply. Perform 3 breath cycles. Inhale fully and exhale fully. With every inhalation and exhalation, you must **feel the air touching the roof** of your palate in your mouth. This is how you will always breathe in meditation, the right way, where you feel the air touching the roof of your palate. Breathe-in to count 1...2...3...4 and similarly, Breathe-out to count 1...2...3...4. Become aware this way.

Exercise #2

Breathe slowly and deeply. Perform 3 breath cycles. Inhale fully and exhale fully. **Breathe through your belly**, consciously bloating your belly as you inhale, and then contract your belly as you exhale. Feel the rising and falling of your belly with each breath. Breathe-in to count 1...2...3...4 and similarly, Breathe-out to count 1...2...3...4. Become aware this way.

Exercise #3

Breathe slowly and deeply. Perform 3 breath cycles. Inhale fully and exhale fully. **Breathe-in without bloating your belly**. Keep your belly firm. Fill up your lower chest and upper chest and feel the difference between breathing like this and breathing from your belly in the earlier step. This is the way you will breathe in the remainder of the exercises. Breathe-in to count 1...2...3...4 and similarly, Breathe-out to count 1...2...3...4. Become aware this way.

The right way to breathe in meditation and the way you will breathe in the remaining exercises is - with every inhale and exhale feel the air touching the roof of your palate, and breathe in without bloating your belly.

Exercise #4

Breathe slowly and deeply. Perform 3 breath cycles. Inhale fully and exhale fully. Breathe-in without bloating your belly. **Feel the air going in and out of your nostrils**; cold air coming in and hot air going out. Breathe-in to count 1...2...3...4 and similarly, Breathe-out to count 1...2...3...4. Become aware this way.

Exercise #5

Breathe slowly and deeply. Perform 3 breath cycles. Inhale fully and exhale fully. Breathe-in without bloating your belly. **Feel the sensations in various parts of your body** as you breathe; in your head, arms, legs, shoulders, back and feet. Breathe through your whole body. Breathe-in to count 1...2...3...4 and similarly, Breathe-out to count 1...2...3...4. Become aware this way.

Exercise #6

Breathe slowly and deeply. Perform 3 breath cycles. Inhale fully and exhale fully. Breathe-in without bloating your belly. As you breathe, **anchor your attention at the point between your eyebrows**; the spot of the third eye. Stay in the spot as you breathe. Breathe-in to count 1...2...3...4 and similarly, Breathe-out to count 1...2...3...4. Become aware this way.

Exercise #7

Breathe slowly and deeply. Perform 3 breath cycles. Inhale fully and exhale fully. Breathe-in without bloating your belly.

Hear the sound of your breath. Hear the sound "Saaa..." as you inhale, and the sound "Haaa...." as you exhale. Breathe-in to count 1...2...3...4 and similarly, Breathe-out to count 1...2...3...4. Become aware this way.

Exercise #8

Breathe slowly and deeply. Perform 3 breath cycles. Inhale fully and exhale fully. Inhale as usual, but when you exhale, with the mouth closed, **make a humming sound** "Hummmm...". Feel the vibrations in your head and body. Breathe-in to count 1...2...3...4 and similarly, Breathe-out to count 1...2...3...4. Become aware this way.

Exercise #9

Breathe slowly and deeply. Perform 3 breath cycles. Inhale fully and exhale fully. In this exercise you will **HOLD your breath for 4 seconds** after every inhalation and after every exhalation. The breath cycle will look like this: Inhale 1...2...3...4, Hold 1...2...3...4, Exhale 1...2...3...4, Hold 1...2...3...4 The holding pattern, the pauses, are important aspects of breathing meditation, and most of the yogic breathing exercises will require you to apply the holding and retention of breath. Breathe-in to count 1...2...3...4 and similarly, Breathe-out to count 1...2...3...4. Become aware this way.

Exercise #10

Breathe slowly and deeply. Perform 3 breath cycles. Inhale fully and exhale fully. In this exercise you will **breathe via ALTERNATE NOSTRILS**: breathe in via the right nostril and breathe out via the left nostril. This means that as you breathe in, the left nostril is closed and right is open. And when you breathe out, the right nostril is closed and the left is open.

The alternate nostril breathing pattern is one of the most fundamental forms of yogic breathing. The breath cycle looks like this:

Block the left nostril, keep right open, breathe in via right.

Block right nostril, in the same moment open left, breathe out via left.

To operate the opening and closing of nostrils, use your right-middle finger to press upon and block the left nostril and breathe in via the right. And use your right thumb to press upon and block the right nostril and breathe out via the left. This way breathing might be made a little challenging for beginners. Give it a try, nevertheless. See how you feel. Breathe-in to count 1...2...3...4 and similarly, Breathe-out to count 1...2...3...4. Become aware this way.

Exercise #11

This is a **RAPID BREATHING exercise** where you will breathe 1 or 2 breaths per second, and you will repeat the cycle 20 to 30 times. The breaths will be forceful and fast. The emphasis must be on exhalation, on throwing out the air with force, by forcing your diaphragm to contract and expand rapidly. When you forcefully exhale, the inhale happens automatically. And you are still breathing via the nose, not mouth. The breath cycle is: out-in; out-in; out-in…and so on.

Exercise #12

The last exercise in this experiment is that of **Chanting Mantra.** You will simply recite the mantra, the word, the universal cosmic sound AUM, and repeat it 10 times.

Chant AUM out loud at a slow pace. Take a deep breath in 1...2...3...4, then chant "AaaOooMmm" for six counts

1...2...3...4...5...6 (Aaa for two, Ooo for two and Mmm for the last two, in continuation as one sound AUM) and repeat 10 times. Be with the sound and feel the vibrations of the sound in your body, especially across the face, head, throat and chest. Become aware this way.

This concludes the experiment.

Congratulations! You just completed your first meditation practice. The wheel is set in motion. Nothing can stop you now from achieving inner peace and lasting happiness. A journey of a thousand miles begins with a first step and you have taken yours by completing the experiment. I wish you all the success in your personal journey.

Now, before you learn the various breathing exercises detailed out later in this chapter, it is important that (a prerequisite, rather) you first learn and understand the ground rules of meditation practice. Without proper application of these best practices as prescribed in the next segment, your meditation practice will not only be less effective, but also incorrect. So, pay close attention and learn the ground rules by heart.

6.3 - The Ground Rules of Practice (step 2/5)

I cannot stress enough how important it is for you to apply the ground rules prescribed in this segment into your daily meditation practice. These rules are about practicing meditation the right way, with right intention, right attitude and right form. These best practices will enhance the performance of your practice and you will see faster results. I suggest you get into the habit of applying these ground rules from day one of your practice and continue using them every day.

These ground rules relate to four broad categories:

1. Setting intention (Making sankalpa).
2. Attitude, Posture and Best Practices.
2. Correct way to breathe in meditation.
3. Holding and retention of breath.

6.3.1 Setting Intention (Making Sankalpa)

The very first thing, the very first exercise you would perform in your daily meditation practice, is always that of "setting your intention". What this means is, that by using some method, or some sort of a ritual, you get your mind and body ready for meditation. This whole concept was covered in detail in section 3.4.1 and it is one of the six core elements of meditation practice. To recap, the main purpose of this exercise is to position yourself with the right mindset for entering into meditation, getting yourself in the zone, and being able to meditate with genuine intent and full concentration.

It is similar in a way, to give an analogy, to an airplane on the runway positioning itself on the path before take-off. It is also analogous to the stretches and warm up routine most people follow in the world of sports and physical workouts. The same way, setting intention exercise in meditation is the mental stretching and warmup that will get your mind and body ready for a productive meditation session.

In Indian culture there is an age-old custom of "making sankalpa", or setting intention, before starting any new task, a new project, any new undertaking in life, such as a sports competition, an exam, a job interview, surgery, dating, travels, and so on. The Sanskrit word "Sankalpa" (sun+cull+pa) carries multiple meanings - setting intention, determination, goal-setting, commitment, resolve, or prayer. It is actually synonymous to saying your prayers and seeking God's blessings, and has the same power as that of a prayer.

Think of this setting intention exercise as you putting out a wish in the universe and declaring your sincere intention of practicing meditation and finding inner stillness. In return you seek guidance and strength from the universe to support you in your endeavour. In my "SoZo Meditation" program the first - minute is allocated to this exercise of making Sankalpa. Please note that this exercise is not some standard way defined by scriptures in the east on starting your practice.

And in regards to the "How" and "What" to do in this exercise, there is no fixed way or standard format. The way you do it, what you do, is up to you, and you have complete freedom to choose your own method. You may choose a prayer or words to say based on your personal beliefs and preferences. You may say it out loud or quietly in your mind.

So as to make this aspect as clear as possible I share one of my personal methods, the way I perform this exercise. Use this as an example to create your own version.

Sitting in the meditation posture, I inhale for 6 counts, hold for 3 counts, and exhale for 6 counts.

Then I say this prayer out loud "Deva (Lord), I sit in meditation today to reclaim my peace, my freedom, my healing, and my happiness from an imprisoned mind. I sit in meditation to lessen my stress, anxieties and fears. I sit in meditation to unburden my mind and experience the inner stillness. Please grant me success in my daily mission. With greater awareness and with a calm and clear mind I am able to face life's challenges with greater strength and mindfulness. As I go within, I am healing myself. I am finding myself. I am able to acknowledge the impermanent nature of all things, and I am able to let go of the past and feel gratitude for the present. I thus pray to thee and seek your blessings for my practice."

And again, I inhale for 6 counts, hold for 3 counts, and exhale for 6 counts. And then I continue with the next exercise in the "SoZo Meditation" program.

6.3.2 Attitude, Posture and The Right Form

Your progress in meditation greatly depends upon your attitude and the mindset with which you perform your practice. In this respect there are a few things that you should be mindful about and which I detail down in this section.

- Think of meditation as your personalized brain enhancement program, tailor-made to your personal goals of an inward journey, and for your highest benefit. Suspend all your doubts and judgments as you meditate.
- When you sit in meditation, slow down a little, calm down a bit, and try not to rush anything. There is, and there should be nothing waiting for you for the next 12

minutes as you practice "SoZo Meditation". There is nothing more urgent and more important than completing your meditation session. The chores can wait. The kids can wait. The spouse can wait. The TV can wait. The phone can wait. Everything can wait. That is the kind of intention and attitude with which you begin your practice.

- Try to find a clean and quiet spot for your meditation practice, and follow a fixed-time and fixed-place routine as far as possible (I covered this aspect in chapter 4). It would also be nice to create your own meditation room, or a cozy corner, with clean surroundings, nice decor, with a meditation cushion or a mat, and place some fresh flowers and plants to create a calming effect, and you may play some background instrumental music.
- Bring your attention inside you. Bring your attention to the in-breath and out-breath. Instead of thinking about staying focused for the next 12 minutes, just think about staying focused on the current breath. One breath at a time as it comes and departs. Welcome your in breath with love and attention, and with same love and attention say goodbye to your out-breath. Then welcome the next in-breath.
- Smile. Meditation is not a serious activity. It is quite an enjoyable activity with great powers. So, wear a half-smile like the Buddha himself. The half-smile symbolizes joy, intention, balance, evenness of mind, wisdom, compassion and awareness.
- While doing breathing exercises, no strain should be felt in the facial muscles, eyes, ears, neck, shoulders, chest, belly, thighs, or feet.[3] The thighs and arms should be

relaxed deliberately since they are unconsciously tensed while sitting for long periods of time.

- Sitting down with folded legs might be quite uncomfortable for beginners. You may experience pain, twitches, itches, or cramps. Just observe the discomfort the best as you can and try not to react or change anything. If it gets too uncomfortable to ignore, however, give yourself permission to scratch, move, or change your posture, and then return to breathing as swiftly as possible.
- Do not critically judge your performance, or somebody else's. There is a reason it's called "practice" and we are not pursuing perfection. It's an ongoing journey where you try to be a little bit better today than you were yesterday. And think about your practice as a game of archery: out of several hundred attempts hitting the target, you may hit the bull's eye only a few times. That's good enough. With regular practice you will hit more and miss less, gradually moving inside, from the outer rings toward the center. It's exactly the same principle in meditation and meditation practice.

- The mind wanders all the time. That is what the mind is habituated to do. The mind will return to thinking thoughts and you won't even notice as this happens unconsciously. Don't be frustrated about losing your focus. Don't panic. Just return back to breathing as soon as you notice you were lost and continue your meditation.

- Don't compare your performance and progress with other people. Your comparison is only with yourself. Build your practice slowly and gradually. One day at a time. Be focused and let nothing distract or discourage you. And control your impulse to share your experience on social media. Everybody will be better off that way. There is nothing to brag about in meditation.

6.3.3 The Correct Way to Breathe in Meditation

- In meditation, always breathe via the nose, not mouth.
- Refer to the yogic breathing technique described in chapter 3.
- As you breathe, feel the air touching the roof of your mouth's palate on its way in and on its way out. It's like breathing from the back of your throat. Feel the cold air going in and the hot air going out. Become aware this way.
- Breath is your anchor, be with the breath, and make it the object of your focus.
- When you inhale, inhale fully, filling up your lungs and upper chest to the brim. Do not strain yourself. Inhalation must be continuous where the entire chest cavity from lowered diaphragm to the highest point of the chest in the region of collar bone is expanded with a uniform movement. Importantly, do not bloat the abdomen.

- When you exhale, exhale fully, emptying your lungs and abdomen of air to the point where you contract your belly a little to the point where you feel a little pinch in your belly button. Keep a firm grip on the abdomen and relax the diaphragm gradually.
- The shift between inhalation and exhalation must be smooth and not jerky. Try to maintain an even and slow rhythm in breathing. Try to maintain an even ratio between in-breaths and out-breaths.
- Acquire the mental idea of rhythm and pay attention to the rhythm of your breathing.
- Try to hear the sound of your breath, the in-breath making a "Saaaa..." sound, and the out-breath making a "Haaaa..." sound. You may also try making a humming sound "Hummm..." during exhalation.
- Never force your breath, except in the rapid breathing exercise.

6.3.4 Holding And Retention of Breath

- The holding and retention of breath after inhalation and exhalation is a common feature in yogic breathing-meditation, and quite an important one. After you inhale completely, you hold-retain your breath for a few seconds before you exhale. And the same way, after you exhale completely, you hold-retain your breath for a few seconds before you inhale again.
- I use the terms "in-hold" for holding-retention after inhale and "ex-hold" for holding-retention after exhale.
- Beginners should not attempt holding-retention until normal breathing is mastered (refer to 6.3.3). In yogic

terminology the terms used for in-hold is "antara kumbhaka" and for ex-hold is "bahya kumbhaka".

- Also, a thorough mastery of in-hold is essential before trying and applying the ex-hold.
- If the holding-retention after every breath cycle becomes harder, then the practitioner may consider mixing up the normal pattern with the holding pattern. For example, 10 breath cycles could be broken down into: 2 normal + 2 holding + 1 normal + 1 holding + 2 normal + 2 holding.
- Ideally, and this is for seasoned practitioners, the unit of holding-retention should be 1/2 of the unit of inhalation and exhalation. For example, the holding pattern breath-cycle would ideally look like this: Inhale 1,2,3,4,5,6 ----- Hold 1,2,3 ----- Exhale 1,2,3,4,5,6 ----- Hold 1,2,3.
- No strain should be felt in the body when applying holding-retention. The shift between breathing and holding must be smooth and without jerks. It is important to maintain a good and even rhythm in your breathing.
- Persons suffering from eye or ear problems, or with weakened heart or lung conditions should avoid applying holding-retention.[3]

6.4 - Energy Locks (aka Bandhas) - (EL)

I explained the concept of Prana in the third chapter as the vital force and vital energy. In yogic breathing you bring in an enormous amount of prana into your system which, when regulated and controlled, can be used more efficiently. The method of controlling, redirecting, and holding Prana inside your body by contracting muscles in the throat, abdomen, groin, and other areas is known as "Bandha(s)", a Sanskrit term, pronounced Bun+Dhā. In this book I refer to this process as "Energy Lock(s)" for simplicity purposes.

Author B.K.S Iyengar has explained the concept of Energy Locks in his book 'Light on Yoga' as follows- when electricity is generated, it is necessary to have transformers, conductors, fuses, switches and insulated wires to carry the power to its destination. Without these controls the electricity generated would be lethal. Similarly, when Prana is made to flow via breathing, during meditation in a meditator's body, it is equally necessary for him to employ 'Energy Locks' to prevent the dissipation of energy and carry it across the body without causing any damage.

The way you implement or apply Energy Locks is quite simple. Each form of Energy Lock is nothing but a posture in which a certain body part, or certain area on your body, is contracted. There are three main Energy Locks that you will use and apply in your meditation practice: (1) Neck Energy Lock - where you contract muscles in your neck, (2) Root Energy Lock - where you contract the lower abdomen and (3) Fly Energy Lock - where you contract both the lower and upper abdomen. I will explain each one in detail in this section.

These Energy Locks are easy to learn and practice- however, an improper technique and form may cause undesirable effects on your body and mind. My advice for the beginners is to skip applying Energy Locks for the first sixty to ninety days. Once you master the base practice and the fundamental skills of breathing, only then you may consider implementing the Energy Locks.

What's more, in Pranayama (meditation) we don't just breathe in a large amount of Prana. According to Yoga philosophy, the object of Pranayama is to arouse 'Kundalini,' the divine cosmic force, in our body. The Kundalini is an enormous amount of power residing in your body that has not been drawn upon at all and is impatiently waiting for the wakeup call. It is symbolized as a coiled and sleeping serpent lying dormant in the lowest nerve center at the base of the spinal column (the Muladhara Chakra). This latent energy has to be aroused and made to go up the spinal column, piercing the chakras up to the highest chakra located on the top of your head. The Kundalini is aroused by the action of yogic breathing and use of Energy Locks.

6.4.1 Neck Energy Lock (NEL)

This Energy Lock in traditional terms of Yoga is known as 'Jalandhara Bandha'(pronounced as Jal+unn+dhāra Bun+dhā).

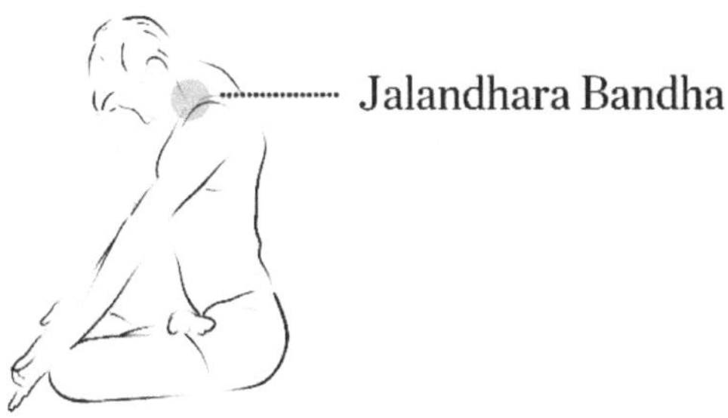

The neck and the throat are contracted and the chin is made to firmly rest on the chest in the notch between the collarbones and the top of the breastbone. You Breathe-in and Breathe-out holding this posture for the entire length of your breathing exercise. Initially, it might be a little hard for you to hold on to this posture for more than a few minutes at a stretch, but with practice things will get easier. Eventually this will become your default posture for all your breathing meditation exercises.

NEL regulates the flow of blood and Prana to the heart, glands in the neck and the head together with brain.[3]

NEL can be applied during the entire breathing cycle, both during inhalation and exhalation, and also during the holding of breath, in-hold and ex-hold.

6.4.2 Root Energy Lock (REL)

This Energy Lock in traditional terms of Yoga is known as 'Mula Bandha'. And Mula (pronounced as Moola) means root, source, origin.

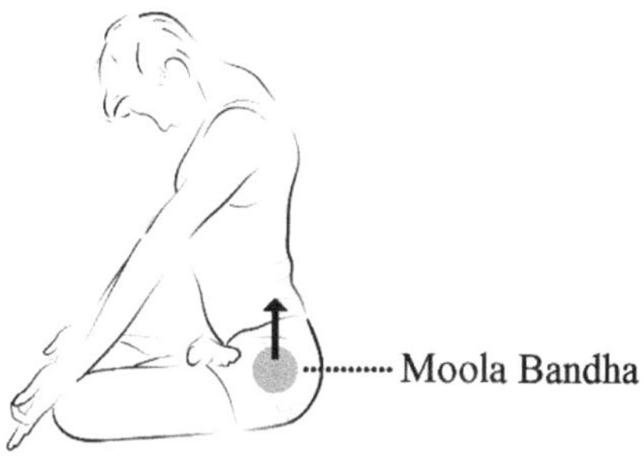

The region between the lower abdomen between the navel and the anus and genitalia is contracted towards the spine and pulled up towards the diaphragm. While practicing REL, the meditator attempts to reach the true source of all creation and the goal is to restrain the mind conditioning, senses, intellect and the ego.

REL can be applied ONLY during the holding pattern and not during inhalation and exhalation. The REL must be attempted first during the in-hold, and only when it is mastered, that it can be attempted during the ex-hold.

6.4.3 Fly Energy Lock (FEL)

This Energy Lock in traditional terms of Yoga is known as 'Uddiyana Bandha'. The word Uddiyana (pronounced as Ood+e+yana) means flying up like a great bird of Prana through the chakras.

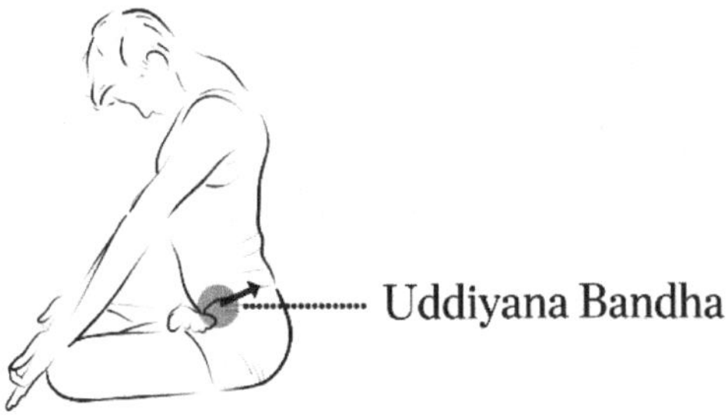

The process is to lift the diaphragm high up the thorax and pull the abdominal organs against the back and towards the spine. The entire region from anus to the diaphragm up to the sternum and thorax (all abdominal organs) is pulled back towards the spine and lifted up high.[3]

FEL must be applied ONLY in the ex-hold. It must never be applied during breathing and the in-hold.

FEL exercises and massages the diaphragm, abdominal organs, and heart muscles.

6.5 - Yogic-Breathing Exercises (Step 3/5)

In this book and in the "SoZo Meditation" program that I prescribe, I have included only FIVE of the most essential yogic-breathing exercises. Again, and I have repeatedly mentioned that- not hundreds of complex forms and types but only a handful of the most fundamental meditation workouts are included in the book. It is important that as a beginner you master these workouts and stay with the program for six months at least, before trying other more intense and complex forms of meditation.

You must remember that meditation is about doing less and patience is your friend. Meditation is not a get-rich-quick kind of phenomenon. It is not a one-day affair. It's an ongoing process where effort is renewed every single day with the rising sun and you build your practice one day at a time. The process of becoming a meditator has to UNFOLD and which happens slowly but surely after an extended period of practice. Also remember that the knowledge and application of the "ground rules" covered in section 6.3 is greatly important and directly impacts the quality and effectiveness of your practice.

The FIVE Yogic-Breathing Exercises included in the "SoZo Meditation" Program are:

1. Vitalizing Breath (code VT) — Slow and Deep breathing, 3-5 breaths per minute.
2. Engine Breath (code EN) — Fast and Shallow breathing; 30-60 breaths per minute.
3. Solar Energy Breath (code SE) — Slow and Deep breathing, inhale via right nostril and exhale via left nostril.

4. Nerve Cleaning Breath (code NC) --Slow and Deep breathing, alternate nostrils, switching sides.
5. Deep Connection Breath (code DC) --- Slow and Deep breathing, alternate nostrils.

Each of the above exercises, except EN, can be performed either in its basic form which I call 'Base-Practice', or it could be performed by adding a slight variation to the base-practice. **These variations are of four types as noted below.** And so that it is easy to understand the concept of variations I would use a quick analogy of vanilla ice cream- you may pick a cup of plain vanilla ice cream, or top it up with strawberry syrup and/or add chocolate chunks and/or add sprinkles, and so on.

Base-Practice: <BP> --- Without applying retention or Energy Locks

Variation 1: <R> ---With retention, applying in-hold and ex-hold (holding breath after inhale/exhale)

Variation 2: <R><NEL> ---With retention and neck Energy Lock

Variation 3: <R><NEL><REL> --- With retention and neck & root Energy Lock

Variation 4: <R><NEL><REL><FEL> ---With retention, neck & root & Fly Energy Lock

In the segment that follows I provide step-by-step instructions for performing each of the five yogic-breathing exercises. Do not be overwhelmed with the number of steps. In order to make things easy for the beginners I have purposefully detailed out the smallest and the finest aspects of the practice. You are not required to learn these steps by heart. After practicing a couple of times, you will naturally be able to remember the logical sequence. Treat the initial few sessions of your practice mainly to be learning and training sessions. Don't judge your performance. Be intent on following each and every step to the fullest with patience. Feel it in your body. Try and understand the meaning of each step and experience the sensations that follow. Don't rush.

These practices carry great power and the practitioner will undoubtedly experience the great life-changing benefits of meditation. Your relationships are going to improve. Your outlook towards life will be more positive. You will feel you have better control over your emotions. You will feel more energy to do more things, and your mind will be sharper than before. Your anxieties and stresses will disappear. And you are going to experience a great sense of peace and relief.

6.5.1 Vitalizing Breath (VT)

This yogic-breathing technique is derived directly from a traditional form of Pranayama known as 'Ujjayi' (Ooj+Jaa+Yee), meaning victory or triumph. The VT is the process of conquering your mind by filling up your lungs with an immense amount of Prana (the Vital-force). It is one of the most basic and the most common forms of yogic-breathing workout which is practiced by millions of meditators around the world. It is also one of the simplest methods to instantly calm a stressed mind. The immense amount of Prana that you bring into your body by virtue of deep breathing in turn vitalizes and nourishes your body and mind.

Key Points:

- Breathe Slowly, Deeply, Steadily and Fully.
- Breathe at a speed of 3-to-5 breaths per minute.

- **The Breath Cycle is**
- <Breathe-in> <Breathe-out>; <Breathe-in> <Breathe-out>; <Breathe-in> <Breathe-out>; and so on…
- In "SoZo Meditation" program you perform a VT for 3 or 4 minutes.

For advanced practitioners, VT can be done as a separate exercise for about 10 to 15 minutes.

The Variations:

	Code
Base Practice	VT
Variation 1 with retention	VT<R>
Variation 2 with retention, neck EL	VT<R><NEL>
Variation 3 with retention, neck EL, root EL	VT<R><NEL><REL>
Variation 4 with retention, neck EL, root EL, Fly EL	VT<R><NEL><REL><FEL>

Steps:

- Turn off the phone and keep it away for a few minutes.
- Observe the ground rules for - attitude, posture and concentration (as described in 6.3.2).
- Sit comfortably in the posture of your choice (see 3.4.3).
- Gently close your eyes.
- Always begin with the exercise of setting your intention for ONE minute (as described in 6.3.1 and 3.4.1).
- After setting intention you are ready to begin the breathing cycle.
- Perform the breath cycle for the specified amount of time as noted in the "SoZo Meditation" program.
- Breathe Slowly, Deeply, Steadily and Fully.

- When you apply variations, observe ground-rules for retention and EL (as described in 6.3.4 and 6.4.)
- Observe the ground rules for breathing (as described in 6.3.3)

a. Breathe via the nose, not mouth.
b. When you inhale, inhale fully up to the brim.
c. When you exhale, exhale fully, empty your lungs.
d. The switch between inhale and exhale must be smooth and not jerky.
e. As you breathe, feel the air touching the roof of your palate.
f. Invite your breath to slow down a little, become a little bit deeper.
g. Don't push too hard and don't strain yourself.
h. Don't bloat your abdomen while breathing.
i. Mind should be absorbed in hearing the sound of the air passage, in-breath (Saaa...), out-breath (Haaa...).
j. Maintain a good rhythm in breathing. You develop greater control with regular practice.
k. Center your attention at a point between the eyebrows to control wandering of the mind.

6.5.2 Engine Breath (EN)

This yogic-breathing technique is derived directly from a traditional form of Pranayama known as 'Bhastrika' (bha+stree+kaa), meaning the bellows used in a furnace to forcefully draw the air in and out of the furnace. The EN is the process in which you use the vigorous force of your breath to generate high energy of a furnace, and you burn your problems, worries and anxieties in this fire. When you breathe forcefully, the sound and intensity of your breath is similar to the sound of a powerful steam engine of a train, and hence the term "Engine Breath”. While the VT is synonymous to a marathon, the EN is synonymous to a fifty-meter sprint. With a strong force you release all your tensions, anxieties, resentments, and thrust it all out of your mind and body to experience great calmness and peace.

Key Points:

- Breathe Fast and Shallow with force.
- Breathe forcefully at a speed of 30 to 60 breaths per minute.
- **The Breath Cycle is**
- <Breathe-out> <Breath-in>; <Breathe-out> <Breathe-in>; <Breathe-out> <Breathe-in>; and so on…
- In “SoZo Meditation program” you perform EN for 2 or 3 minutes
- For advanced practitioners, EN can be done as a separate exercise for about 5 to 7 minutes
- If anytime during the cycle you feel dizzy or tired then immediately either reduce your speed or stop
- Some people may feel emotional during or after performing this exercise as the forceful breathing may bring up some old hurts and old emotions trapped inside your body. It is quite normal, however. If you feel restless at any point during the workout then slow down or stop at once.

The Variations

Base Practice (No retention and Energy Locks)

Steps:

1. Turn off the phone and keep it away for a few minutes.

2. Observe the ground rules for - attitude, posture and concentration (as described in 6.3.2).
3. Sit comfortably in the posture of your choice (see 3.4.3).
4. Gently close your eyes.
2. Always begin with the exercise of setting your intention for ONE-minute (as described in 6.3.1 and 3.4.1).
3. After setting intention you are ready to begin the breathing cycle.
4. You start the breath cycle with breathing out. When you exhale with a force the inhale will happen automatically. Think of the breath cycle as exhale-exhale-exhale…
5. When you exhale, pull your diaphragm and abdomen toward the spine with force. The emphasis is on throwing out the breath.
6. Perform the breath cycle for the specified amount of time as noted in the "SoZo Meditation" program.
7. Keep your body lucid. You may rock a little while performing forceful breathing. This is normal.
8. Think like this - with each exhale you are throwing out all your negativity, your worries, your problems and your anxieties; and with each inhale you are breathing in peace, positivity, health and happiness.
9. Observe the ground rules for breathing (as described in 6.3.3)
   a. Breathe via the nose, not mouth.
   b. As you breathe, feel the air touching the roof of your palate.
   c. Your mind should be absorbed in hearing the sound of the air - like the sound of a steam engine train.

d. Maintain a good rhythm in breathing. You develop greater control with regular practice.
e. Center your attention at a point between the eyebrows to control the wandering of the mind.

6.5.3 Solar Energy Breath (SE)

This yogic-breathing technique is derived directly from a traditional form of Pranayama known as 'SuryaBheda', meaning piercing the sun. This is one of the many alternate nostril breathing techniques. The human body is a miniature universe in itself (recall the 'two-worlds' described at the beginning of the book). With every breath the solar and lunar energy is said to flow through the two main nerve centers (known as 'Nadi', naa+dee, in Sanskrit) via the two nostrils, and move down to the base of the spine crossing through various Chakras (described in 3.4.3).

The right nostril is the Nadi of the Sun, while the left nostril is the Nadi of the Moon. In between them, is the Nadi of fire - the Prana. By stimulating the forces of the sun and the moon, one at a time, you ignite the fire and bring in the energy synonymous to the energy of piercing the sun.

The main benefit of alternate nostril breathing technique is balance and clarity. "Our bodies operate most efficiently in a state of balance, between action and relaxation. And this balance is influenced by the nasal cycle. The right nostril is deeply connected with the sympathetic nervous system, while the left nostril is connected with the parasympathetic nervous system. The right nostril breathing speeds up circulation, the body gets hotter, increases cortisol levels, heart rate, and blood pressure. The left nostril has opposite effects, lowers temperature, blood pressure, and reduces anxiety."[64] SE meditation is known to increase digestive power, soothe and invigorate nerves, and cleanse the sinuses.[3]

Key Points:

- Inhale via right nostril; Exhale via left nostril; Apply retention after inhale only (the in-hold).
- Breathe Slowly, Deeply, Steadily and Fully.
- Breathe at a speed of 3-to-5 breaths per minute.

The Breath Cycle is

Cycle1: <Breathe-in from right> <in-hold> <Breathe-out from left>;

Cycle2: <Breathe-in from right> <in-hold> <Breathe-out from left>; and so on…

- In "SoZo Meditation" program you perform SE for 2 or 3 minutes.

For advanced practitioners, SE can be done as a separate exercise for about 10 to 15 minutes.

The Variations:

	Code
Base Practice for SE includes in-hold by default	SE or SE<R>
Variation 1 with neck EL	SE <NEL>
Variation 2 with neck EL, root EL	SE <NEL><REL>
Variation 4 with neck EL, root EL, Fly EL	SE <NEL><REL><FEL>

Steps:

1. Turn off the phone and keep it away for a few minutes.
2. Observe the ground rules for-attitude, posture and concentration (as described in 6.3.2).
3. Sit comfortably in the posture of your choice (see 3.4.3).

4. Gently close your eyes.
5. Always begin with the exercise of setting your intention for one minute (as described in 6.3.1 and 3.4.1).
6. After setting intention you are ready to begin the breathing cycle.
7. Perform the breath cycle(s) for the specified amount of time as noted in the "SoZo Meditation" Program.
8. Inhaling from only one nostril (right nostril) will require you to block the other (left nostril). And similarly, exhaling from only one nostril (left nostril) will require you to block the other (right nostril).
9. To operate the opening and closing of nostrils use your right hand, bend it at the elbow and bring the palm over to your nose. You can find plenty of reference pictures and videos on internet on how-to
10. You will use your right thumb to open/close the right nostril.
11. You will use your little finger and the ring finger together to open/close the left nostril.
12. Begin by placing your right thumb next to your right nostril, not touching but hanging on the side, and press the little and ring fingers on the tip of the left nostril, gently but completely closing it shut.
13. Begin breath cycle - Inhale slowly, deeply and fully from the right nostril.
14. Inhaling via one nostril instead of two can be a little difficult in the beginning. You may feel a little pressure in your nasal passage, but this is normal. Things will ease up with regular practice.
15. At the end of inhalation from the right and before you begin to exhale from the left, you apply retention (in-hold). In order to do that you block the right nostril by

pressing on its tip with the right thumb so that now both the nostrils are blocked. You now perform an in-hold retention for 3 to 4 seconds before you begin to exhale.

16. After retention, in order to exhale from the left nostril, you release the little and ring fingers to open it and in the same instant keep the right nostril blocked and pressed under your thumb.
17. End the breath cycle - Exhale slowly, deeply and fully from the left nostril.
18. Repeat the breath cycle (steps 12 to 17) for a specified amount of time as noted in the "SoZo Mediation" program.
19. The length of inhale and exhale should roughly be the same. Initially the inhalation might be longer than exhalation, but with regular practice proper rhythm and control can be achieved.
20. The length of retention can be increased to up to five seconds or more as you develop greater control.
21. When you apply variations, observe ground-rules for retention and EL as described in 6.3.4 and 6.4.
22. Observe the ground rules for breathing (as described in 6.3.3)
    a. Breathe via nose, not mouth.
    b. When you inhale, inhale fully up to the brim.
    c. When you exhale, exhale fully, empty your lungs.
    d. The switch between inhale and exhale must be smooth and not jerky.
    e. As you breathe, feel the air touching the roof of your palate.
    f. Invite your breath to slow down a little, become a little bit deeper.
    g. Don't push too hard and don't strain yourself.

h. Don't bloat your abdomen while breathing.
i. Mind should be absorbed in hearing the sound of the air passage, in-breath (Saaa...), out-breath (Haaa...).
j. Maintain a good rhythm in breathing. You develop greater control with regular practice.
k. Center your attention at a point between eyebrows to control wandering of the mind.

6.5.4 Nerve Cleansing Breath (NC)

This yogic-breathing technique is derived directly from a traditional form of Pranayama known as 'Nadi-Shodhana', pronounced as show+dhā+na, meaning cleansing of nerves.[44] The 'Nadi', pronounced as na+dee, is a Sanskrit term meaning artery, nerve or a vein through which the vital-force, the Prana, is carried to various parts of the body. And 'Shodhana' is a Sanskrit term meaning cleansing or purification. When the flow of prana is abundant and unobstructed it will bring internal cleaning of mind and body, and you will experience a great sense of well-being and rejuvenation. NC is a very powerful technique which when practiced the right way can bring immense benefits of physical and mental health for the practitioner.

The ancient Vedas say there are 72,000 nadis in the body. The nadis often become contaminated with thought forms of lower and negative energy. These can become toxic, and when they do, our experience of living is substantially lowered, leading to physical and emotional dysfunction. Therefore, it is important to purify, cleanse, correct and balance the nadis.

Key Points:

- Inhale via right nostril and Exhale via left; then reverse direction: Inhale via left nostril and Exhale via right.
- Breathe Slowly, Deeply, Steadily and Fully.
- Breathe at a speed of 2 to 4 breaths per minute.

The Breath Cycle is

a. Exhale via right nostril	--- this is a preparatory step
b. Inhale via right nostril	--- cycle 1 begins here
c. Exhale via left nostril	
d. Inhale via left nostril	
e. Exhale via right nostril	--- cycle 1 ends here
f. Inhale via right nostril	--- cycle 2 begins here
g. Exhale via left nostril	
h. Inhale via left nostril	
i. Exhale via right nostril	-- cycle 2 ends here
j. Inhale via right nostril	-- cycle 3 begins here

and so on...

- In "SoZo Meditation" program you perform NC for 2 or 3 minutes.

For advanced practitioners, NC can be done as a separate exercise for about 8 to 10 minutes.

The Variations:

	Code
Base Practice	NC
Variation 1 with retention	NC<R>
Variation 2 with retention, neck EL	NC<R><NEL>
Variation 3 with retention, neck EL, root EL	NC<R><NEL><REL>
Variation 4 with retention, neck EL, root EL, fly EL	NC<R><NEL><REL><FEL>

Steps:

1. Turn off the phone and keep it away for a few minutes.
2. Observe the ground rules for-attitude, posture and concentration (as described in 6.3.2).
3. Sit comfortably in the posture of your choice (see 3.4.3).
4. Gently close your eyes.
5. Always begin with the exercise of setting your intention for one minute (as described in 6.3.1 and 3.4.1).
6. After setting intention you are ready to begin the breathing cycle.
7. Perform the breath cycle(s) for the specified amount of time as noted in the "SoZo Meditation" program.
8. Inhale/Exhale from the right-only nostril will require you to block the left nostril. And similarly, Inhale/Exhale from left-only will require you to block the right nostril.
9. To operate the opening and closing of nostrils use your right hand, bend it at the elbow and bring the palm over to your nose. You can find plenty of reference pictures and videos on internet on how-to
10. You will use your right thumb to open/close the right nostril.
11. You will use your little finger and the ring finger together to open/close the left nostril.
12. Begin by placing your right thumb next to your right nostril, not touching but hanging on the side, and press in the little and ring fingers on the tip of the left nostril, gently but completely closing it shut.
13. Begin the breath cycle.

14. Breathe-out of the right nostril (this is the preparatory stage 'a' in the cycle noted above).
15. Inhaling via one nostril instead of two can be a little difficult in the beginning. You may feel a little pressure in your nasal passage, but this is normal. Things will ease up with regular practice.
16. Breathe-in via right-only nostril (this is stage 'b' in the cycle noted above).
17. To exhale from the left-only nostril you must close the right nostril and open the left nostril. To achieve this switch, you release the little and ring fingers from the left nostril to open it and in the same instant press the thumb on the tip of the right nostril to close it shut.
18. Breathe-out via left-only nostril (this is stage 'c' in the cycle noted above). ‘
19. Breathe-in via left-only nostril (this is stage 'd' in the cycle noted above).
20. You now need to exhale from the right nostril, which means you must close the left nostril and open the right nostril. To achieve this switch, you release the thumb from the right nostril to open it and in the same instant press the little and ring fingers on the tip of the left nostril to close it shut.
21. Breathe-out via the right nostril (this is stage 'e' in the cycle noted above).
22. This completes one cycle of NC.
23. Repeat the breath cycle (steps 16 through 21) for a specified amount of time as noted in the “SoZo Meditation” program.
24. The length of inhale and exhale should roughly be the same. Initially the inhalation might be longer than

exhalation, but with regular practice proper rhythm and control can be achieved.

25. The length of retention can be increased to up to five seconds or more as you develop greater control.
26. When you apply variations, observe ground rules for retention and EL as described in 6.3.4 and 6.4.
27. The retention and Energy Locks should not disturb the rhythm and quality of breathing. If things get a little difficult with retention, try to reduce the duration of in-hold and ex-hold, or better, apply retention on alternate cycles.
28. Observe the ground rules for breathing (as described in 6.3.3)
    a. Breathe via the nose, not mouth.
    b. When you inhale, inhale fully up to the brim.
    c. When you exhale, exhale fully, empty your lungs.
    d. The switch between inhale and exhale must be smooth and not jerky.
    e. As you breathe, feel the air touching the roof of your palate.
    f. Invite your breath to slow down a little, become a little bit deeper.
    g. Don't push too hard and don't strain yourself.
    h. Don't bloat your abdomen while breathing.
    i. Mind should be absorbed in hearing the sound of the air passage, in-breath (Saaa...), out-breath (Haaa...).
    j. Maintain a good rhythm in breathing. You develop greater control with regular practice.
    k. Center your attention at a point between the eyebrows to control wandering of the mind.

Caution:[3]

Persons suffering from high blood pressure or other heart problems should not apply retention. Practice without applying in-hold and ex-hold. Persons suffering from low blood pressure may want to avoid ex-hold and apply only in-hold. Keep your body relaxed during performing NC meditation. You must not feel any tension in your neck, shoulders, arms or thighs.

6.5.5 Deep Connection Breath (DC)

This yogic-breathing technique is derived directly from a traditional form of Pranayama known as 'Anuloma', (pronounced as anoo+loma), meaning going with the grain or going with the natural rhythm of the things. DC is the process of establishing a deep connection with your inner world by aligning your mind and body with the natural rhythm of the universe. When your energy vibrations synchronize with the vibrations of universal energy, merging into the cosmic sound of AUM, then you experience deeper intuition, creativity, intelligence, and grand awareness.

This exercise has similar benefits to VT and NC.

Key Points:

- Breathe Slowly, Deeply, Steadily and Fully
- Inhale via both nostrils and exhale via right; then reverse: Inhale via both nostrils and exhale via left.

• **The Breath Cycle is**

Cycle1 : <Inhale via Both nostrils><in-hold><Exhale via Right nostril> + <Inhale via Both nostrils><in-hold><Exhale via Left nostril>

Cycle 2: <Inhale via Both nostrils><in-hold><Exhale via Right nostril> + <Inhale via Both nostrils><in-hold><Exhale via Left nostril>

and so on...

- The base practice contains in-hold only and not the ex-hold; meaning you perform only the in-hold (holding breath upon inhalation) and you don't perform the ex-hold (holding breath after exhalation).
- In "SoZo Meditation" program you perform DC for 2 or 3 minutes.

For advanced practitioners, DC can be done as a separate exercise for about 8 to 10 minutes.

- If anytime during the cycle you feel dizzy or tired, immediately either reduce your speed or stop.

The Variations:

	Code
Base Practice (With in-hold only)	DC
Variation 1 with neck EL	DC<NEL>
Variation 2 with neck EL, root EL	DC<NEL><REL>
Variation 3 with neck EL, root EL, fly EL	DC<NEL><REL><FEL>

Steps:

1. Turn off the phone and keep it away for a few minutes.
2. Observe the ground rules for-attitude, posture and concentration (as described in 6.3.2).
3. Sit comfortably in the posture of your choice (see 3.4.3).
4. Gently close your eyes.
5. Always begin with the exercise of setting your intention for one minute (as described in 6.3.1 and 3.4.1).

6. After setting intention you are ready to begin the breathing cycle.
7. Take a deep breath in via both nostrils the same way as you would breathe in VT exercise in VT breathing.
8. At the end of inhalation perform the in-hold for 3 to 4 seconds (or more).
2. In order to exhale from the right-only nostril you'd block the left nostril and breathe-out via right. Follow the same method for opening and closing nostrils as described for SE (solar energy) breathing.
3. At the end of exhalation unblock the left nostril so that both nostrils are now open for inhalation.
4. Inhale again via both nostrils as you'd do in VT breathing.
5. At the end of inhalation perform the in-hold for 3 to 4 seconds (or more).
6. In order to exhale from the left-only nostril you'd block the right nostril and breathe-out via left. Follow the same method for opening and closing nostrils as described for SE (solar energy) breathing.
7. At the end of exhalation unblock the right nostril so that both nostrils are now open for inhalation.
8. Repeat steps 7 through 14 for the specified amount of time noted in the "SoZo Meditation" program.
9. When you apply variations, observe the ground rules for retention and EL as described in 6.3.4 and 6.4.
10. Observe the ground rules for breathing similar to the VT breathing (and as described in 6.3.3)

6.6 - Relaxation Techniques (Step 4/5)

The core concept of "Relaxation" was covered in chapter 3 (3.4.6). In this section I describe two of the popular relaxation exercises:

a. Yog Nidra

b. Progressive Relaxation

These two techniques are quite similar in nature and help relax the whole mind and body, and reduce stress and anxiety. In both these exercises you navigate your attention across each muscle group or each part of your body, moving from one area to another, from head to toe or from toe to head, progressively, in a particular order. A detailed guidance and step-by-step instructions on how to perform these exercises is included in this segment.

6.6.1 The Yog Nidra Deep Relaxation Technique [YN]

The Sanskrit word Yog means Yoga, and Nidra (pronounced Nee+dra) means sleep. The concept is that by using this technique you can produce the same level of relaxation (in a wakeful state) as produced by the deep-sleep state. This technique is greatly effective in relaxing your mind and body, and is especially recommended to be used after a rigorous physical workout or an intense meditation session.

Starting at your toes, you progressively move your attention upward towards your head, mentally scanning one body part at a time. The process of this relaxation technique is that you focus your attention on one specific area of the body, a muscle group, become aware of it and immediately, in the same instant, withdraw your attention off that spot and focus it on the next body part, scanning in sequential progression. By mentally touching each part, each area of the body from head to toe, you are able to release tension and strain from your whole body and induce the feeling of great relaxation and calmness of body and mind.

The Steps to Follow

1. As shown in the picture below, lie flat on your back, full length like a corpse. Keep your hand away from your body, palms up. Keep the heels together and toes apart forming a V-shape. If keeping heels together is uncomfortable then space it out with a small gap between them.

2. Maintain slow and steady breathing without much effort.
3. The lower jaw should hang loose and not be clenched.
4. Gently close your eyes.
5. Take a couple of deep breaths and relax.... Slow down.... Relax....
6. The navigation and scanning sequence that you will follow in focusing your attention is as below:

   Right Leg >> Left Leg >> Lower Abdomen >> Right Arm >> Left Arm >> Upper Abdomen >> Chest>> Neck >> Face >> Head

7. As you navigate, keep your body light. Imagine you are slowly getting submerged in water; or imagine yourself falling freely from the sky. Let gravity take over and just release yourself.
8. From the next step onward, focus your attention on each of the body parts in sequence, one by one, without skipping. You withdraw your attention immediately and in the same instance you focus your attention on the next body part in the sequence. By a rough estimate it may take only about 1 second per body part, and the entire scanning will take at most about 60 to 90 seconds. Remember that the focus-withdrawal-focus action happens quickly, within an instant. You are only mentally touching the body part and diffusing the energy from that area, thus enabling relaxation.

   Start Scanning

9. Right foot >> Toes >> Top of the foot >> Sole >> Ankle >> Shin >> Calf Muscles >> Knee >> Top of thigh >> Bottom of thigh >> Whole right leg >>
10. Left foot >> Toes >> Top of the foot >> Sole >> Ankle >> Shin >> Calf Muscles >> Knee >> Top of thigh >> Bottom of thigh >> Whole left leg >>
11. Whole Right and Left legs together, simultaneously >>
12. Waist area >> Groin region >> Butt >>
13. Right palm >> Fingers >> Wrist >> Forearm >> Elbow >> Upper Arm >> Whole right arm >>
14. Left palm >> Fingers >> Wrist >> Forearm >> Elbow >> Upper Arm >> Whole left arm >>
15. Whole Right and Left arms together, simultaneously >>
16. Lower back >> Belly region >>

17. Chest >> Upper back >> Right shoulder >> Left shoulder >> Whole area from Groin to Shoulders>>
18. Neck >> Back of the neck >>
19. Face >> Chin >> Lips >> Mouth >> Cheeks >> Jaw >> Nose >> Eyes >> Ears >> Forehead >> Whole Face >>
20. Top of the Head >> Scalp >>
21. Whole body from Toes to Head >> Whole body from Head to Toes
22. End Scanning
23. Now just relax and do nothing. Breathe slowly, normally and lie down like this for another minute or two.
24. Gently turn on one side and take support with your elbow and arm, lift yourself up into a sitting position. Don't open your eyes yet.
25. Vigorously rub your palms together to warm them up a bit and then lay them on your eyes for a couple of seconds.
26. Gently open your eyes.

You will notice that the navigation and scanning sequence is quite logical and you don't have to really memorize it. You may simply navigate one area at a time starting at the toes and moving up progressively to end at the top of your head.

6.6.2 Flex and Release Technique (FR)

The Yog Nidra technique of the past has manifested in many different types and variations in the modern times. There are dozens of varieties offered around the world. Across these variations, however, the fundamental principle remains the same, and which is about progressive relaxation. It is about navigating your awareness all across your body, relaxing one body part at a time.

The Flex and Release technique is one such variation. In this exercise you essentially tighten and relax each muscle group in your body. The main difference between this exercise and Yog Nidra is that in YN you are only "mentally" touching a body part and withdrawing your attention off that part, while in PR you "physically" tighten and relax a particular muscle group. Progressively navigating from toe to head, or head to toe, you focus on a muscle group, flex it, hold it tight for few seconds, and release the tension before moving on to the next muscle group.

As shown in the picture below, lie flat on your back, full length like a corpse. Keep your hand away from your body, palms up. Keep the legs apart a bit forming a V-shape.

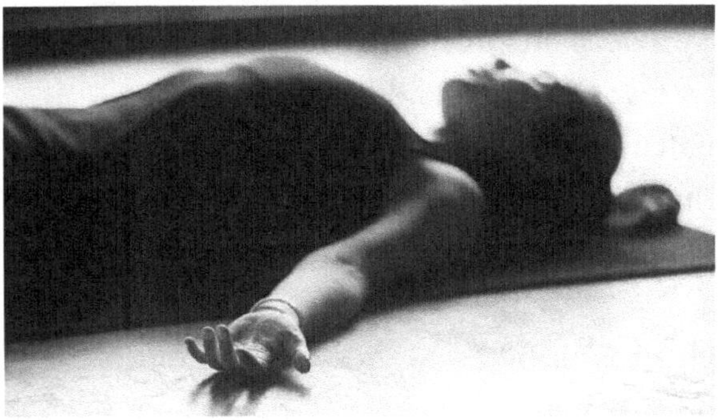

Steps

1. Take 5 deep breaths. Don't strain yourself. Become aware of your breath.
2. Take a deep full breath quickly, and then exhale slowly. As slowly as you can. And repeat this three times.
3. Take a deep breath, starting from the top of your head. Tighten the whole face area, then hold as long as you can, release and relax.

4. Take a deep breath, scrunch up your forehead and hold for 5 sec. Let go.
5. Take a deep breath, tighten your mouth & jaw and hold for 5 sec. Let go.
6. Open and stretch your mouth as wide as you can, hold for few seconds and then let go
7. Take a deep breath and release all tension in your face.
8. Take a deep breath, pull your shoulders up toward your head and tighten all muscles in your neck. Hold for a few seconds and then let go.
9. Take a deep breath, tighten your arms and hands. Hold for a few seconds and then let go.
10. Take a deep breath, push your arms into the floor. Hold for a few seconds and then let go.
11. Take a deep breath, tighten your chest and abdomen. Hold for a few seconds and then let go.
12. Tighten back, lower back. Hold for a few seconds and then let go.
13. Tighten stomach area. Hold for few seconds and then let go.
14. Tighten your butt and groin area. Hold for few seconds and then let go.
15. Tighten upper legs, thighs. Hold for few seconds and then let go.
16. Tighten your calves, feet and crunch up your toes. Hold for few seconds and then let go.
17. Take a deep breath, tighten your whole body again... let go.
18. Do a body scan, head, face, neck, shoulders, arms, chest, abdomen, back, legs, feet... Let go.
19. Now just relax and do nothing. Breathe slowly, normally and lie down like this for another minute or two.

20. Gently turn on one side and take support with your elbow and arm, lift yourself up into a sitting position. Don't open your eyes yet.
21. Vigorously rub your palms together to warm them up a bit and then lay them on your eyes for a couple of seconds.
22. Gently open your eyes.

CHAPTER 7
THE "SOZO MEDITATION" PROGRAM: YOUR GAME PLAN

7.1 - Daily 12-minute Scalable Technique And Program

It is with careful consideration and research, taking into account all that has been discussed in this book so far, that I have developed a simple yet comprehensive "SoZo Meditation": Daily 12-Minute Scalable Program for the beginners and new seekers of meditation.

This is it. This is your game plan. And honestly, this is all you really need to get started.

I reiterate, there is no need for hundreds of different types and complex forms of meditation workouts which only make things harder and not easier. Meditation practice is not a multi-variety show. Meditation is not a get-rich-quick kind of phenomenon. Meditation is the art of doing less and less. Meditation is a science of slowing down. Meditation is about repeating the same things over and over and over and over again. It is the repetition of successive efforts which bring the desired results of quieting the mind, lowering the number of thoughts, reducing the mind's clutter, and resting your intellect from calculating, analysing, jumping from one mental disturbance to another.

Let's dive into the program without any delay.

The Key Points of the Program

- You will perform FIVE meditation exercises every day which are timed as below for a total duration of 12 minutes:

  Total 12 minutes

First exercise	1 minute
Second exercise	3 minutes
Third exercise	2 minutes

Fourth exercise	2 minutes
Fifth exercise	4 minutes

- The first exercise will always be that of "Setting Intention". The fifth exercise will always be that of "Chanting Mantra". And the three exercises in between will be the Yogic-Breathing exercises.
- Repeat the same sequence every single day with a small variation added every two weeks or every month. In the beginning, perform the base practice of each exercise with no variations. The variations will be introduced slowly and gradually as you master the base practice. We are not going to rush things here. The whole point of meditating in the first place is to slow down a little. The progress happens in phases, one step at a time.
- Once you master the base practice, I introduce and add "Retention", as described in 6.3.4. Once you master retention, I introduce and add Neck Energy Lock (NEL). Once you master NEL, I introduce and add Root Energy Lock (REL). And finally, once you master REL, I introduce and add the Fly Energy Lock (FEL). Again, the program and your practice will grow in phases, which is the right way of practicing meditation.
- The "SoZo Meditation" program is a 6-Month program which can be scaled and customized based on your progress. Importantly, the program is bundled into a unique format noted below.

Program Outline

The exercise schedule is broken down in the following format.

Month 1	First 30 Days	First 15/30 Days		
		Second 15/30 Days	(add Retention)	
Month 2 & 3	Next 60 Days	First 30/60 Days	(add NEL)	Odd Day
				Even Day
		Second 30/60 Days	(add REL)	Odd Day
				Even Day
Month 4	Next 30 Days		(add FEL)	Odd Day
				Even Day
Month 5 & 6	Next 60 Days	Cycle of 4 (Day 1, Day 2, Day 3, Day 4)		

- Lastly, I include a clear strategy with multiple options on how you may scale up your practice beyond six months and continue your progress.

You should have no doubts in your mind as to whether or not this program will work for you and whether or not you will experience the benefits of meditation. That is guaranteed to happen as long as you can stick with the program and put in 12 minutes of daily effort. That is a promise. And it will happen a lot sooner than later. Don't let anybody tell you otherwise and distract you from your practice and your goals. Don't listen to your friends trying to make fun of you or discourage you in any way. Be firm, be earnest and be sincere in your practice. And remember, a 12-minute practice performed with full commitment and focus is a million times more productive than practicing for 30 minutes or longer where you are unfocused and uninterested. So, get onboard with confidence.

Your life is about to change, my friends.

7.2 - The Program Table (Step 5/5)

LEGEND

Code	Description	Section#
SI	Setting Intention	6.3.1, 3.4.1
VT	Vitalizing Breath	6.5.1
EN	Engine Breath	6.5.2
SE	Solar Energy Breath	6.5.3
NC	Nerve Cleansing Breath	6.5.4
DC	Deep Connection Breath	6.5.5
CM	Chanting Mantra	3.4.5
R	Retention and Hold	6.3.4
EL	Energy Locks	6.4
NEL	Neck Energy Lock	6.4.1
REL	Root Energy Lock	6.4.2
FEL	Fly Energy Lock	6.4.3
YN	Yog Nidra Relaxation	6.6.1
FR	Flex Release Relaxation	6.6.2

FIRST 30 DAYS (1ST MONTH)

First 15 of 30 Days > Base Practice

P1-01

#	Duration	What To Do	Code
1	1 Minute	Setting Intention	SI
2	3 Minutes	Vitalizing Breath base practice	VT
3	2 Minutes	Engine Breath base practice	EN
4	2 Minutes	Solar Energy Breath base practice	SE
5	4 Minutes	Chanting Mantra	CM

Second 15 of 30 Days> Introduce Retention

P1-02

#	Duration	What To Do	Code
1	1 Minute	Setting Intention	SI
2	3 Minutes	Vitalizing Breath with Retention	VT<R>
3	2 Minutes	Engine Breath base practice	EN
4	2 Minutes	Solar Energy Breath base practice	SE
5	4 Minutes	Chanting Mantra	CM

+ Twice a week – Yog Nidra (YN) or Flex and Release (FR))

NEXT 60 DAYS (2ND AND 3RD MONTH)

First 30 of 60 Days> 2nd Month> Introduce and add NEL

P1-03

Odd Day

#	Duration	What To Do	Code
1	1 Minute	Setting Intention	SI
2	3 Minutes	Vitalizing Breath with Retention, NEL	VT<R> <NEL>
3	2 Minutes	Engine Breath base practice	EN
4	2 Minutes	Nerve Cleaning Breath base practice	NC
5	4 Minutes	Chanting Mantra	CM

+ Twice a week – Yog Nidra (YN) or Flex and Release (FR)

P1-04

Even Day

#	Duration	What To Do	Code
1	1 Minute	Setting Intention	SI
2	3 Minutes	Vitalizing Breath with Retention, NEL	VT<R> <NEL>
3	2 Minutes	Engine Breath base practice	EN
4	2 Minutes	Solar Energy Breath base practice	SE
5	4 Minutes	Chanting Mantra	CM

+ Twice a week – Yog Nidra (YN) or Flex and Release (FR)

Second 30 of 60 Days > 3rd Month > Introduce and add REL

P1-05

Odd Day

#	Duration	What To Do	Code
1	1 Minute	Setting Intention	SI
2	3 Minutes	Vitalizing Breath with R, NEL, REL	VT<R> <NEL> <REL>
3	2 Minutes	Engine Breath base practice	EN
4	2 Minutes	Nerve Cleansing Breath with Retention	NC<R>
5	4 Minutes	Chanting Mantra	CM

+ Twice a week – Yog Nidra (YN) or Flex and Release (FR)

P1-06

Even Day

#	Duration	What To Do	Code
1	1 Minute	Setting Intention	SI
2	3 Minutes	Vitalizing Breath with R, NEL, REL	VT<R><NEL><REL>
3	2 Minutes	Engine Breath base practice	EN
4	2 Minutes	Solar Energy Breath with NEL	SE<NEL>
5	4 Minutes	Chanting Mantra	CM

+ Twice a week – Yog Nidra (YN) or Flex and Release (FR)

NEXT 30 DAYS (4TH MONTH)

4th Month>Introduce and add FEL

P1-07

Odd Day

#	Duration	What To Do	Code
1	1 Minute	Setting Intention	SI
2	3 Minutes	Vitalizing Breath with R, NEL, REL, FEL	VT<R><NEL><REL><FEL>
3	2 Minutes	Engine Breath base practice	EN
4	2 Minutes	Nerve Cleansing Breath with R, NEL, REL	NC<R><NEL><REL>
5	4 Minutes	Chanting Mantra	CM

+ Twice a week – Yog Nidra (YN) or Flex and Release (FR)

P1-08

Even Day

#	Duration	What To Do	Code
1	1 Minute	Setting Intention	SI
2	3 Minutes	Vitalizing Breath with R, NEL, REL, FEL	VT<R><NEL><REL><FEL>
3	2 Minutes	Engine Breath base practice	EN
4	2 Minutes	Solar Energy Breath with NEL, REL	SE<NEL><REL>
5	4 Minutes	Chanting Mantra	CM

+ Twice a week – Yog Nidra (YN) or Flex and Release (FR)

NEXT 60 DAYS (5TH AND 6TH MONTH)

P1-09

Cycle Of Four (Apply Retention and All Energy Lock)

#	Duration	Day 1	Day 2	Day 3	Day 4
1	1 Minute	SI	SI	SI	SI
2	4 Minutes	VT	VT	VT	VT
3	3 Minutes	EN	NC	SE	DC
4	4 Minutes	CM	CM	CM	CM

+ Twice a week – Yog Nidra (YN) or Flex and Release (FR))

7.3 - Guidance for The Next 6 Months

After successfully completing the 6 months program you will naturally develop an increased capacity for a longer-duration practice and intense meditation workouts. In order to switch things up and advance your progress in meditation you may choose something from the various options listed below.

1. Continue doing P1-09 for additional six months. Doing less is doing more, and there is absolutely no problem in sticking with the same routine for a longer period.

2. If you could spare a little bit of extra time for meditation then increase the duration of practice from 12 minutes to 15 minutes, and perform the "cycle of four" with timings specified in P1-10 below.

P1-10

Cycle Of Four (15 minutes)

#	Duration
1	1 Minute Setting Intention (SI)
2	4 Minutes Vitalizing Breath
3	4 Minutes Solar Energy Breath or Nerve Cleansing Breath
4	6 Minutes Chanting Mantra

3. Consider practicing "SoZo Meditation" twice daily. I personally follow the morning and evening routine with my first practice around 10am and the second around 5pm. And I practice Yog Nidra every night.

4. Chanting Mantra can be performed by itself as a separate exercise and which I strongly recommend doing. Practice “SoZo Meditation” in the morning and in the evening add a separate ten-minute CM exercise.

5. In regards to the duration of practice the general rule of thumb is- longer the practice, the greater the benefits. For those who can perform longer practice I prescribe two new "SoZo Meditation" programs, P1-11 (20-Minutes) and P1-12 (30 Minutes).

P1-11
20-Minute Program
Cycle of THREE

#	Duration	Day 1	Day 2	Day 3
1	1 Minute	SI	SI	SI
2	4 Minutes	VT	VT	VT
3	4 Minutes	NC	SE	DC
4	3 Minutes	EN	EN	EN
5	8 Minute	CM	CM	CM

+ Thrice a week YN/FR

P1-12
30-Minute Program
Cycle Of Three

#	Duration	Day 1	Day 2	Day 3
1	1 Minute	SI	SI	SI
2	5 Minutes	VT	VT	VT
3	5 Minutes	NC	SE	AN
4	5 Minutes	DC	NC	SE
5	4 Minutes	EN	EN	EN
6	10 Minutes	CM	CM	CM

+ Thrice a week YN/FR

Final Word

That is it, my friends. I have said enough, and I have done so with the honest intent to point you in the right direction. Meditation practice is a royal road to well-being. I hope this book will serve to support you and inspire you. The journey is yours to take. The possibility that you will undergo your own powerful transformation exactly the way I did mine with the help of meditation practice, inspired me to write this book in the first place. This is your journey of reclaiming your peace and happiness from an imprisoned mind. Use the power of breath and meditation to bring a positive transformation in your lives. You can do it. Commit yourself to the inner work of freedom. The ancient practice of meditation is really about a very simple thing- quieting the mind and realizing freedom. Your life will be more beautiful and you will be free. It is my sincere hope that you will discover and experience the supreme benefits of meditation practice in your life. May you find your inner peace just as I found mine.

Om Shantih, Shantih, Shantih.

ACKNOWLEDGEMENTS

First and foremost, I want to thank my partner in crime, my wife Madhura. Without her extraordinary and unwavering support, this book would not have seen the light of day.. From the very first moment when I shared my idea with her, she was on board, and she has been my main support throughout the book writing process. Being incarcerated, I was working under severe limitations - without computer, printer, scanner, software, digital storage, email attachments, and limited communications, limited contact, dependency on postal mail, and so on.

Madhura helped me with, well, everything – typing, printing, scanning, mailing, handling outside communication on my behalf, talking with publishers, receiving and forwarding mails, emails, finding information, and so much more. And at the same time, in my absence, she was single-handedly managing everything at the home front, managing her job, house tasks, kids, parents, bills, payments, everything. She would still somehow find time for me and my book in addition to wholeheartedly providing emotional and financial support. Thank you Madhura, for being such a wonderful partner all along.

Another person without whom this book would not have been possible is my best buddy, Salil Sawale. He has a degree in Mechanical Engineering, but chose his career in the creative profession as a copywriter. Salil is a creative genius and currently works at one of the top Ad agencies in Bangalore, India. During the early stages of my book when it was a raw manuscript, Salil helped me with a first round review and editing. His feedback and his little tweaks tightened the loose ends, significantly improving the overall tone.

In the later stages of the three-year long project, Salil helped with the cover design and editing the text content for the cover page. His creative eye gave life to the beautiful design. During this period we had numerous zoom calls to discuss his feedback and suggestions. Importantly, Salil also found and facilitated a communication focal point for me, who would communicate with the publishers on my behalf. Given the limitations, it would have been virtually impossible for me to communicate with the publishing team without external help. Thank you, Mitraa, for your kindness and patience, and for being such an incredible friend.

I would also like to thank Salil's wife, Aarti, who helped with typing a couple of chapters for me. Thanks, Sis.

I would also like to thank Isha, my elder daughter, for her help in typing a few chapters for me in the early stages of the book, and especially for compiling and sharing my feedback with the editor on the changes and corrections to the manuscript. During the initial stages, changes in the manuscript was a long-drawn process, thanks to my limited access to tools. I would type my edits into a text-only Email App on my tablet. And because of a 1500 characters limit per email my feedback was scattered across multiple emails. Isha would compile those changes into a word file and then either implement those edits into the manuscript herself, or forward it to my editor. It was a massive effort. Thank you, Ishu. I love you and I am so proud of you.

Two other people in my family who helped me a great deal were - my sister Dipali Ghodake and her brother-in-law

Nileaysh Ghodake. Nileaysh is a managing partner of Typographica Press Services, located in the city of Pune, India. They both helped a great deal during the entire length of my book project by facilitating professional typing, editing, and cover design services. With their help I was able to complete the first draft of my manuscript which I could send out to publishers. Thank you, Nileaysh, for your brilliant support. And thank you, Dipali, for your patience and for your love.

I would like to thank Muskan Raj, my communications coordinator and focal point for the publisher's communication. Without her help, it would have been impossible for me to communicate with the publishing team and cross the finish line. In fact, it was Muskan who researched and found BlueRose Publishers for me. During the process of finding publishers she forwarded my proposal to several publishing houses and literary agents in India. And ultimately she was instrumental in landing the deal for me with BlueRose. Muskan has a very positive go-getter attitude and she is an excellent communicator. Thank you, Muskan, for your incredible professionalism and support.

A special note of gratitude to BlueRose Publishers, and the team at the publishing house – Shruti and Sakshi- Publication managers, Nancy- Sales Team, Daksh- Cover design lead, Dhruvi- Editing coordinator, Priyavar, Tanya – Formatting Lead and all other talented folks on the team, who finally gave shape to my dream. It was wonderful to finally find someone who shared my passion, and acknowledged my vision to see it to fruition. Your belief in my work, and the long hours you put in to coordinate with me, have been instrumental in getting this book out.

There is a popular saying that does the rounds in American prisons, that prisons have some of the best creative talents in the world. And I experienced it up close to know that it's true. During my time here, I came across some brilliant artists and I have seen their incredible artwork - canvas art, freehand drawings, portraits, calligraphy, sketches, wall murals, tattoo art, and much more.

I would like to thank one such artist, Devin Smith (aka Skinny), my first cellmate upstate, for converting my original concept for the cover design into an extraordinary piece of art. He took my crudely made ordinary drawing, and converted it into a beautiful artwork. He is an African American artist who only had heard about Buddha and Buddhist religion, but had never really seen or drawn a Buddha image. The calming Buddha face you see on the cover has been created by him, entirely from my rudimentary description. Thank you, buddy, for a splendid job.

I would also like to thank two other fellow inmate friends of mine. Thanks to R. Murphy Jr. for sharing his book-writing story and planting the seed in my head to write my own. And thanks to Michael Baynard, for typing my manuscript multiple times on his typewriter during the initial stages of the project. Thank you for your patience.

As one famous scientist once proclaimed, "If I have seen further, it is by standing on the shoulder of giants." I would like to again thank all the great authors I referenced in my book. I am a mere speck of dust in comparison to these mighty mountains of wisdom. Their works, their words, their wisdom, and their insights inspired me to think, to write, and to create. Thank you all, for energizing my spiritual revolution.

REFERENCES

Author's Note

My head bows down in respect to the brilliant authors and their works listed here. I have been greatly inspired by their words of wisdom in writing my book. Any success this book may ever find would belong to these great authors and any shortcoming belongs to me and only me.

I have written this book in prison. Needless to say, being incarcerated comes with its own challenges and limitations. These limitations restricted my ability to communicate with the outside world and my access to resources for research which are unrestricted to the general public, such as online material and books. I had no computer, no internet, no typewriter, no digital storage, limited access to the prison library, limitations on books I could order, restricted email use, restrictions on receiving printed material, limited contact with family and friends…the list goes on.

I understand this is done because an incarcerated individual cannot have same privileges and provisions as that of a person in the free world. The actual writing process, with multiple rounds of editing, revisions, sending and receiving, was an arduous pen-paper based undertaking.

The reason I am talking about these limitations is not to complain about the system, but to highlight how it possibly impacted my ability to provide detailed references to the texts I used from the works of other authors. I take notes when reading a book, and over my long stay at county prison I had a big stack of notes taken from multiple books. A lot of these notes got stolen and misplaced at county prison where incidents of stealing property were commonplace. I have, nevertheless, done my best to include all the references wherever applicable and wherever possible. If I have missed any link or citation, it is due to the limitations noted above and I apologize in advance. It is never my intention to pass off someone else's work as mine. In fact, it is my firm belief that I have been able to achieve my objective by standing on the shoulders of giants and that I am deeply thankful for their part in transforming this book from dream to reality.

Finally, to everyone who picked up this book, I thank you from the bottom of my heart. I wrote it for all those who are struggling, who have been sucker punched by life's adversities and still have the incredible courage to keep going. I see you and reach out to you, because if prison has taught me one thing, it's that people will change you. This book is an adventure, and I'm happy you're coming aboard.

Happy Journey!

Sources

1. Andrew Newberg and Robert Waldman. (2009). *How God Changes Your Brain: Breakthrough Findings from a Leading Neuroscientist*. Ballantine Books.
2. Deepak Chopra. (1991). *Unconditional Life: Discovering the Power to Fulfill Your Dreams*. Bantam Books.
3. B.K.S Iyengar. (1966). *Light on Yoga.* George Allen and Unwin.
4. David Brooks. (2019). *The Second Mountain: The Quest for a Moral Life*. Penguin Random House LLC
5. Rajshree Patel. (2019). *The Power of Vital Force: Fuel Your Energy, Purpose, and Performance with Ancient Secrets of Breath and Meditation.* Hay House Inc.
6. Thich Nhat Hanh. (1999). *The Heart of Buddha's Teaching*. Rider and Co.
7. Eknath Easwaran. (2006). *Strength in the Storm: Transform Stress, Live in Balance, and Find Peace of Mind. Eknath Easwaran*. Jaico Publishing House.
8. Eknath Easwaran. (2016). *Passage Meditation.* Nilgiri Press.
9. Eknath Easwaran. (2007). *The Bhagavad Gita.* Nilgiri Press.
10. Eknath Easwaran. (2009). *The Upanishads.* Jaico Publishing House.
11. Michio Kaku. (2014). *The Future Of The Mind.* Doubleday.
12. Timothy Ferris. (1992). The Mind's Sky. Bantam Books.

13. Mendi.io (2023) Did you know that the average human brain generates 45 thoughts per minute? Medium.com. https://medium.com/@Mendi.io/did-you-know-that-the-average-human-brain-generates-45-thoughts-per-minute-92a8c3514d5a

14. Bo Lozoff. (1998). We Are All Doing Time. Human Kindness Foundation.

15. Eckhart Tolle. (2004). The Power of Now: A Guide to Spiritual Enlightenment. New World Library.

16. Jon Kabat-Zinn. (2005). Wherever You Go There You Are. Hyperion.

17. Joseph Murphy. (2015). The Power of Your Subconscious Mind. Amazing Reads.

18. Ajhan Chah. (2007). Clarity Of Insight. The Sangha, Wat Nong Pah Pong. Retrieved from https://www.ajahnchah.org/book/Clarity_Insight1.php

19. Gil Fronsdal. (2008). The Issue at Hand: Essays on Buddhist Mindfulness Practice. Insight Meditation Center.

20. Thannisar Bhikku (Geoffrey DeGraff). (2013). With Each & Every Breath- A Guide to Meditation. Retrieved from https://www.dhammatalks.org/Archive/Writings/Ebooks/WithEachAndEveryBreath_210603.pdf

21. Ajhan Chah. (2011). Seeing The Way, Vol. II. Aruna Publications.

22. Thich Nhat Hanh. (2005). Happiness: Essential Mindfulness Practices. Parallax Press

23. Judith Hensen Lasater. (2015). Living Your Yoga. 2nd Edition. Shambhala Publications Inc.

24. Jiddu Krishnamurti. (2016). The Awakening of Intelligence. KFI Publications.

25. Viktor Frankyl (2010). Man's Search for Meaning: The classic tribute to hope from the Holocaust. Rider & Co.

26. Daniel Amen. (2018). Feel Better Fast and Make It Last. Tyndale House Publishers Inc.

27. Marlo Morgan. (2004). Mutant Message Down Under. Harper Perennial.

28. Phakyab Rinpoche and Sofia Stril-Rever. (2017). Meditation Saved My Life: A Tibetan Lama and the Healing Power of the Mind. New World Library.

29. Loch Kelly. (2019). The Way to Effortless Mindfulness. Sounds True Inc.

30. Annie Besant. (2002). An Introduction to Yoga. The Project Gutenberg

31. A.P. Mukerji. (2004). Doctrine and Practice of Yoga. The Project Gutenberg.

32. Swami Paramahansa Yogananda. (1998). Autobiography of A Yogi. Yogoda Satsanga Society of India.

33. Yogi Ramacharaka. (2004). The Hindu Yogic Science of Breath. The Project Gutenberg

34. Tinker Hawkeye. (2013). Buddhist Boot Camp. HarperOne.

35. C.S. Lewis. (2004). The Inspirational Writings of C.S. Lewis. Thomas Nelson Publishers.

36. Bradley Nelson. (2019). The Emotion Code. St. Martin's Essentials.

37. Rick Warren. (2014). The Purpose Driven Life. Zondervan.

38. Alex Lickerman. (2002). The Undefeated Mind: On the Science of Constructing an Indestructible Self. Health Communications Inc.

39. Laird Hamilton and Julian Borra. (2019). Life Rider. Rodale Books.

40. Roy Masters. (1988). Beyond The Unknown. Foundation of Human Understanding.

41. Will Durant. (2011). Our Oriental Heritage: The Story of Civilization. Vol. I. Simon and Schuster.

42. Dennis N.T. Perkins, et al.. (2000). Leading The Edge: Leadership Lessons from the Extraordinary Saga of Shackleton's Antarctic Expedition. AMACOM.

43. Yuval Noah Harari. (2015). Sapiens. Harper Perennial.

44. Jose Luis Stevens. (2014). Awaken The Inner Shaman: A Guide to the Power Path of the Heart. Sounds True Inc.

45. Gabor Maté with Daniel Maté. (2022). The Myth of Normal: Trauma, Illness and Healing in a Toxic Culture. Penguin Random House.

46. Gabor Maté with Daniel Maté. (2010). In The Realm of Hungry Ghosts: Close Encounters with Addiction. North Atlantic Books.

47. Swami Shri Satchidananda. (2020). Yoga Sutras of Patanjali, 9th Printing. Integral Yoga Publications.

48. Yung Pueblo. (2022). Lighter: Let Go of the Past, Connect with the Present, Expand the Future. Harmony.

49. Leroy Hood And Nathan Price. (2023). The Age of Scientific Wellness: Why the Future of Medicine is Personalized, Predictive, Data-Rich, and in Your Hands. The Belknap Press.

50. Darlene Santore. (2023). The Art of Bouncing Back: Find Your Flow to Thrive at Work and in Life Any Time You're Off Your Game. McGraw Hill.

51. Ari Wallach. (2022). Longpath: Becoming the Great Ancestors Our Future Needs-An Antidote for Short-Termism. HarperCollins Publishers.

52. Nancy Allison. (1998). The Illustrated Encyclopedia of Body-Mind Disciplines. The Rosen Publishing Group Inc.

53. Caroline Myss. (1997). Why People Don't Heal and How They Can: A Practical Programme for Healing Body, Mind and Spirit. Three Rivers Press.

54. Roger N. Walsh and Frances Vaughan. (1980). Paths Beyond Ego: The Transpersonal Vision. TarcherPerigee.

55. Dawson Church. (2018) Mind to Matter. Hay House Inc.

56. OSHO. (2019). The Buddha Said. Watkins Publishing.

57. Julie Rosenberg. (2017). Beyond The Mat: Achieve Focus, Presence, and Enlightened Leadership through the Principles and Practice of Yoga. Da Capo Lifelong Books.

58. Dr.Terry A. Gordon. (2012). No Storm Lasts Forever. Hay House Inc.

59. Anthony Silard. (2012). The Connection. Atria Books.

60. Daniel Amen. (2023). Change Your Brain Everyday. Tyndale House Publishers

61. Dr.Wayne Dyer. (2004). The Power Of Intention: Learning to co-create your world your way. Hay House, Inc.

62. Sadhguru. (2021). KARMA: A Yogi's guide to crafting your destiny. Penguin Ananda.

63. Sadhguru. (2016). Inner Engineering: A Yogi's guide to joy. Penguin Ananda.

64. Robin Casarjian. (1995). House Of Healing: A prisoner's guide to inner power and freedom. Lionheart Press.

65. James Nestor. (2020). Breath: The new science of a lost art. Riverhead Books.

66. Gaylon Ferguson. (2009). Natural Wakefulness: Discovering the wisdom we were born with. Shambhala Publications Inc.

67. Claudia Black. (2024). Undaunted Hope: Stories from trauma, depression and addiction. Central Recovery Press.

ABOUT THE AUTHOR

Nikhil is a first-time author and an all-time explorer. He is an avid reader and a seasoned meditation practitioner and teacher. Born and raised in a small city in Gujarat State in Western India, Nikhil is a dedicated family man, having been married for over twenty years and a proud father of two.

With a degree in Computer Engineering and Masters in IT Management, he has decades of experience managing the ERP/HRI software implementation projects in India, Middle East, and USA. He worked with giant corporations in Technology and Oil & Gas sector, and he is a certified Project Management professional and certified SPHR. His career prowess is only eclipsed by his globetrotting adventures. With a passport full of stamps and a mind full of memories, he has traversed the seven continents, gaining insights and imbibing perspectives from diverse cultures.

After living and working in the UAE for nearly two decades, Nikhil migrated to USA, where tragically his life took a detour and he ended up locked-up behind bars. Written from the unlikely setting of a prison cell, this book marks the beginning of his new mission and newfound life's purpose, to help others heal and recover from life's adversities using the transformative powers of meditation practice.